REFUGEES

ANARCHY OR ORGANIZATION?

REFUGEES

ANARCHY OR ORGANIZATION?

BY

DOROTHY THOMPSON

*With an Introduction
by Hamilton Fish Armstrong*

Random House

New York

FIRST PRINTING

D
445
T46

To my friends in exile, amongst them some of the noblest spirits and most gifted minds that I have ever known.

Contents

INTRODUCTION BY HAMILTON FISH ARMSTRONG   ix

FOREWORD   xiii

1. THE PROBLEM   3

2. TWENTIETH-CENTURY MIGRATIONS   13

3. THE JEWISH REFUGEES   56

4. THIS STILL EMPTY WORLD   80

5. TOWARDS A PRACTICAL PROGRAM   92

BIBLIOGRAPHY   123

Introduction

THE PROBLEM of the refugee—political, racial, religious—is as old as man. It becomes acute in every cruel and intolerant age. The present age is cruel and intolerant; and many people who are not either are nevertheless satiated of pity, so that they no longer react to tales of horror and injustice as they once would have done.

Old fires of intolerance which the last generation thought extinguished everywhere except in lands confessedly barbarous are flaming again. And we who still profess to be civilized are enervated by constantly reading and hearing about the repeated victories of the twentieth-century barbarians. We are in bitter need of being reminded that cold-blooded terrorism anywhere is not something to which we can ever become habituated, that we can never accept it as normal. In our own country, individuals, groups, classes and political organizations lapse from civilized standards of conduct every day in the year. The papers of every city and town record those lapses, from Jersey City to San Jose and from Tampa to South Chicago.

But at least our national government has not adopted them as policies of state. It has not imprisoned pastors and priests for being more faithful to God than to the district leader. It does not shoot political and military chiefs for favoring national or international policies different from the official policies of the moment (though perhaps the same as yesterday's, and very likely the same as tomorrow's), or for being more "liberal" or more "conservative," more "red" or more "white" or more "black." It has not instituted two classes of citizens, the lower of which is not entitled to even a pretended protection of any stated law. It does not assert the right to seize the goods of those "second-class" citizens, deny them a livelihood at the same time that it denies them an opportunity to leave under equitable conditions, destroy the homes that have been theirs for generations, and imprison them or throw them penniless into exile.

We need spokesmen who will recall to us that this difference between wrong asserted as right and wrong protested but not yet defeated is complete and irreconcilable. We need spokesmen who will reanimate our pity for the victims of personal and public outrage, wherever perpetrated; who will renew our courage; who will challenge us to demonstrate our intellectual capacity for dealing rationally with the problems which those outrages create, both in social relationships and in international politics.

That is why it was a timely as well as an eloquent note which the State Department sent recently, by President Roosevelt's direction, to some thirty Governments, inviting them to discuss the refugee problem in all its aspects. There need be no secret that the State Department's action was stimulated by the article by Dorothy Thompson which had just been published in the April, 1938, issue of *Foreign Affairs*. It is good that Miss Thompson has agreed to expand the story and carry it further, and particularly that she has specific suggestions to make about procedure, now all-important.

The tasks at hand are both political and philanthropic, but political even more than philanthropic. Dorothy Thompson always cares about what she writes about. This characteristic—calm passion animating a careful marshaling of fact—never was better displayed than in her demonstration, in the pages which follow, of the political significance of the refugee problem. The civilized world must cope with that problem now or admit one more disintegrating defeat.

June 4th, 1938.

HAMILTON FISH ARMSTRONG

Foreword

THIS SMALL BOOK makes no claim to eloquence or literary style. It was written in great haste, under an enormous pressure of other work, simply because it seemed to the author that it *had* to be done. Contemplation of the fate of refugees, awareness of the international social problems which new mass migrations were creating, and apprehension that these problems would increase in virulence unless competently met, wrung from me this effort to formulate the problem and its history, and present, however tentatively, some ideas for meeting it. These ideas did not spring full-fledged from my own imagination. They involved research into what had already been done, investigation of the existing literature on the subject, and consultation with many persons who have had practical experience with the problem from one angle or another.

The author originally aired the problem in the April, 1938, number of *Foreign Affairs,* and it was due to the response from that article, and to the fact that the President of the United States in the same month proposed an international action, that it was thought worth while to elaborate the original article beyond the scope possible for magazine publication.

I am indebted to Countess Waldeck for much assistance in research, especially into the history of the modern refugee problem which she first aired in the April 1937 number of *Foreign Affairs*.

REFUGEES

ANARCHY OR ORGANIZATION?

CHAPTER ONE

The Problem

As I WRITE THIS, the news from Europe is distressing in the extreme. Austria has become a district of Greater Germany. Central Europe is in turmoil, as every small state of the Danube Basin feels the increasing pressure of Nazidom. Great Britain and, following her leadership, France are considering whether—and if so, how—to protect Czechoslovakia, and whether—and if so, how—to save even a modified League of Nations. The Soviet system seems in a state of serious disintegration. The war in Spain continues, to what final denouement we cannot yet foresee. These chaotic situations cannot fail to add to a problem which is already a world headache—that of dispossessed racial and political minorities.

If one side or the other wins the Spanish civil war there will immediately be a forced emigration of political refugees. Every indication from Spain, too, is that both sides are beginning to wish to rid themselves of foreigners, and not all of them can return to the places from which they came. In Germany, more and more Jews are being deprived of the means to continue living in the homes they have had for centuries, while the situation of many Christians, both Protestant and Catholic, is, to say the least, precarious. On the heels of the Nazi victory in Austria there has followed a regime of terror for Jews, for partisans of Dollfuss and Schuschnigg, for still-surviving liberals, for proponents of a Hapsburg restoration and also for Catholics—thus creating a pressing new problem of refugees. Rumania is experimenting with anti-Semitic laws. The Jewish question in Poland has been acute for some years.

In the Danube Basin alone—in Austria, Czechoslovakia, Rumania, Hungary and Jugoslavia—live some two million Jews. There are over three million more in Poland. And these figures do not include Christian converts, or men, women and children of part Jewish blood who under the German Nuremberg laws are assigned to the Jewish community. Austria has many such. There are also many in Czechoslovakia and Hungary. If any more countries fall under Nazi domination, or come under Nazi influence, a further growth of anti-Semitism is certain. Even if they shy away from the

German "Aryan program," because most of these peoples are not Germans at all, but Slavs, or Magyars, or of mixed races other than Jewish; even if King Carol of Rumania proceeds more slowly with his anti-Semitic program than his unfortunate late Prime Minister, Mr. Goga; even if Hungary introduces limited anti-Semitic laws; even if a partly Nazified Czechoslovakia should adopt only an attenuated form of anti-Semitism, millions of Jews nevertheless are in danger of becoming pariahs. And at least a part of them will make every effort to leave their homes to escape starvation.

Since the end of the war some four million people have been compelled by political pressure to leave their homes. A whole nation of people, although they come from many nations, wanders the world, homeless except for refuges which may any moment prove to be temporary. They are men and women who often have no passports; who, if they have money, cannot command it; who, though they have skills, are not allowed to use them. This migration—unprecedented in modern times, set loose by the World War and the revolutions in its wake—includes people of every race and every social class, every trade and every profession: Russian aristocrats and, more lately, Russian technicians;

Italian liberal professors and Austrian Socialist workmen; German individualists of any and every stripe; Monarchists in republics and Republicans in monarchies; priests and radicals; artists and laborers; capitalists and anti-capitalists; the flower of the prosperous Jewish bourgeoisie and the inhabitants of East European half-ghettos; non-conformists of every race and every social, religious and political viewpoint.

The possibility that this number is to be augmented within the immediate future is undeniable. To close one's eyes to it would be ostrichism in an acute form. Realism demands that one must contemplate the fact with more than a horrified humanitarianism. This twentieth-century migration of peoples occurs in a world where there is a new, even if temporary, downward swing in the business cycle; in which many countries have serious unemployment problems which private enterprise alone has been unable to solve; in which every country has erected strong barriers against immigration, whether in the form of quotas or the requirement of work permits which foreigners are in practice unable to obtain; in which government policies of exclusion are supported or even made more rigorous by trade-union demands.

WORLD UNREST INCREASES

This chaotic migration has added prodigiously to world unrest, and not least in those countries that are trying to work out the problems of the modern state along democratic and constitutional lines. The fear of a wave of unselective immigration leads such states to adopt a more extreme nationalism than they would otherwise consider desirable. This in turn increases internal tensions. So it is that we must record the growth of Xenophobia and anti-Semitism in countries which never before were conscious of having a "Jewish problem," or an "alien problem," where, prior to the past five years, the Jews were satisfactorily assimilated to the whole society, and where there is actual underpopulation. The growth must be regarded with alarm, not only for humanitarian reasons but because it contains in itself a germ destructive of the essential principles of democratic society, of any society based on principles other than those of primitive racialism.

If the present strong currents of migration continue to push anarchically upon those states still open to immigrants; if it is now further to be horribly augmented; if it is not consciously directed; if assistance is not furnished to immigrants so that they are sure not to become a burden upon their hosts; if they cannot be turned into definite economic assets—then there is a catastrophe ahead for more than the immigrants and the would-be immigrants.

NO INCLUSIVE AGENCY EXISTS

There is at present in the world no agency handling the problem of political exiles in a comprehensive way. Of the three existing institutions, neither the International Labor Office nor the Nansen International Office, an autonomous body responsible to the League, nor the office of the "High Commissioner for Refugees Coming from Germany," which is only loosely attached to the League, has ever been authorized to consider or deal with the whole question of political and racial exiles. Recently, the Council of the League decided that the field of activities of the Nansen Office should be extended and that after the end of 1938, the Nansen Office and the Office of the High Commissioner for Refugees should be merged into a single organization to be set up for a limited period, to take the place of the two existing organizations, directed by a person designated by the League, this High Commissioner to be assisted by a small staff, comprising neither refugees nor former refugees.

As a matter of fact this will probably prove to be a way of killing off both organizations rather than extending or vitalizing their activities. This commission will be in a position to offer the refugees some legal protection; to facilitate the coordination of humanitarian activities. But the Council Committee of the League which proposed the new plan for international assistance to refugees in a report to the League in May 1938, proposes new economies in administrative expenditure and contemplates no allocation of funds for the relief or settlement of refugees. Nor is the new commission required to report to the League.

Therefore, and in view of the lack of authority from which the League as a whole suffers, and in view of the sabotage against any constructive settlement of the refugee problem, which is exercised by certain members of the League, notably Soviet Russia, it is extremely improbable that any of the League institutions will undertake to deal with the refugee problem on the scale required.

PRESIDENT ROOSEVELT APPEALS

Therefore, the appeal of President Roosevelt for international action to aid political refugees is not only timely, generous and imaginative, but it is extremely necessary—not for the sake of the refugees only, but for the sake of all countries that are anxious to prevent further unrest and economic and social disequilibrium.

Obviously what this action needs is a program and efficient organization to deal with the whole matter.

The moment is not politically inopportune. The very urgency of the European crisis provides arguments for such an agency. An attempt is about to be made to settle the most acute differences between the dictatorial and the democratic powers. That attempt implies some sort of compromise on all sides if it is to have any chance of success.

We ought not to view the problem, complicated as it is, in a spirit of defeatism. Even the anti-Semitic governments are conscious that their anti-Semitism creates internal problems for them. Only through cooperation can they hope to work out the problems they have themselves created.

Too long the refugee problem has been largely regarded as one of international charity. It must be regarded now as a problem of international politics. Actually what prompted the President of the United States to take a hand in it was, no doubt, a keen sense of self-preservation. The world, as it is, is a place of unrest and agitation with desperate people taking desperate measures in the attempt merely to survive. And millions of people wandering more or less aimlessly, and battering at every conceivable door, being passed from frontier to frontier, will certainly do nothing to restore world order.

Nor can any democratic country wash its hands of this problem if it wishes to retain its own soul. The very essence of the democratic principle is humanistic; it involves respect for human dignity and human personality; it implies a revulsion against persecution of individuals; it rejects arbitrary edicts; when its capacity for righteous indignation is exhausted by weariness or by callousness, then the democratic principle will die.

It is perfectly true that the problem has not been created by the democracies but by new forms of government which reject the concepts of law and ethics that still rule the democratic world. The burden is not of our making, but nevertheless it is impossible for us not to accept the burden put upon us, and while opposing the political attitudes which have created it, to try to meet it and deal with it.

We have got to face the reality that liberal democracy is the most demanding of all political faiths, and in the world today the most aristocratic. It is a political philosophy which makes painful demands. That is its price. That is also its glory.

And so a defeatist attitude toward the refugee problem, created by the opponents of democracy, becomes a defeatist attitude toward democracy itself.

CHAPTER TWO

Twentieth-Century Migrations

I HAVE SAID that since the end of the War four million people have had to leave their countries under political pressure.

This new great migration has a precedent only in the great movements of population which took place in the fourth and fifth centuries, when Asiatic peoples began pressing the German tribes southward into the Roman Empire.

In those days the conqueror wandered, and so wandered the conquered—the conqueror fired by his desire for richer lands, the conquered forced from his home by the invader's ferocity. The motive of these early movements of population was the conqueror's: *"Ôte—toi que je m'y mette!"*

These were barbarous times when the strong were always right. But though a thousand years of Christian civilization have developed the noble consciousness of duty toward the weak; though the modern conqueror arises from within instead of intruding

13

from without; though the issue is not land but power: the motive is still the same.

The weak are forced out of their countries by pressure from the strong. Driven out are those who hold political ideas opposed to those of the ruling caste, and those who are of a different race from the national majority. In many cases these citizens are not directly expelled; but the moral, political, and economic pressure brought upon them is such that they prefer the uncertainties of exile to an intolerable life in the homes where they have lived for generations.

STATISTICS ARE INADEQUATE

All statistics about the new great migration are incomplete. Until the Nazi statesmen frankly announced that they intended to rid themselves of their Jews, governments which were engaged in expelling their citizens had a rather shamefaced tendency to understate the number of their refugees, with an eye to the opinion of a humanitarian world. And the immigration countries, unaware that the refugee question was going to develop into a major political problem, did not bother to keep exact statistics as to the refugees' number and economic status.

Moreover, the definition given by League of Nations' agencies to the term "refugee" is so narrow, that their statistics do not reveal the full extent of the new great migration.

According to the official League definition, a Russian refugee, for instance, is "any person of Russian origin who does not enjoy, or no longer enjoys, the protection of the Government of the USSR, and who has not acquired another nationality." All the other categories of refugees are similarly defined—thus excluding all refugees who during the last twenty years have managed to acquire another nationality, but who none the less left home under political pressure.

It is, however, estimated that from 1918 until now 1,500,000 Russians have fled from Soviet Russia; 1,500,000 Greeks from Anatolia and the Turkish provinces; 350,000 Armenians from Asia Minor; 120,000 Bulgarians from Greece; 25,000 Assyrians from Iraq; 150,000 Germans from Germany; 8,000 from the Saar; and a number, at present unknown, of Austrians from Nazified Austria.

But there are additional groups of refugees where numbers are mere guesswork: the Hungarians who fled before the Red Terror and the Hungarians who fled before the White Terror, the Italians who fled from Mussolini, the Spaniards who fled from Primo de Rivera and the Spaniards who fled from the Republic.

It was the good fortune of "the first generation of refugees"—the Russians, Armenians, etc.—to be poured forth into a world that was comparatively willing to receive them. Europe had lost its men in the war. The early twenties were a period of reconstruction. The refugees were used as a reservoir of labor, especially in France where the labor shortage was so acute that they called in Polish and Italian workmen.

This does not mean that the refugee problem was an easy one to tackle even then, or that it ever found a wholly satisfactory solution. The agencies designated to deal with refugees constantly suffered from two chronic ailments: lack of coordination and lack of funds.

THE GREAT NANSEN

There was nobody who felt this lack of coordination and this lack of funds more acutely than the man whose name has become fused with the refugee work done in the last twenty years. This man was the Norwegian, Dr. Fridtjof Nansen. From 1921 until his death in 1930, everything that was done for refugees was instigated and influenced by him.

When the League appointed him High Commissioner for Refugees he was about sixty. He had
behind him the daring life of a North Pole ex-
plorer, rich in activities, experience and lonely ad-
venture. His ice-blue eyes radiated purity and
strength. They were the eyes of a man who for
three years—alone, his fate unknown—had wandered the frozen Polar Zone. Hero, adventurer,
archangel—all in one—he set in motion the imagination of every man, woman and boy. The curiosity
he roused, the authority he enjoyed were immense.
Moreover, his humanitarianism was backed by a
great capacity for practical organization. With un-
tiring energy he succeeded time and again in rous-
ing the inertness of a war-weary world for the
millions whose grim fate it was to wander the earth.

What the whole refugee problem needs today,
more than anything else, is another Nansen—one
man, or a few men, with his simple belief in human
dignity, his faith in human decency, his enormous
sense of personal honor and responsibility and his
confidence in the power of humanity to organize
and mobilize to meet its emergencies.

Nothing in the League Covenant expressly authorized international help for refugees except a
phrase in the preamble stipulating that one of the
League's objects is "to promote international coop-

eration by the maintenance of justice" and Article
23 of the Covenant, which prescribes that "members of the League will endeavor to secure and
maintain fair and humane conditions of labor for
men, women and children, and for that purpose
will establish and maintain the necessary international organizations." But the International Red
Cross and other relief organizations joined in for-
mally requesting the League to take appropriate action. Dr. Nansen's appointment as High Commissioner was the League's answer to this request.

In the first years the High Commissioner was directly responsible to the Council and was not an
officer of the Secretariat. He was assisted by an
Advisory Committee, composed of representatives
of philanthropic organizations, and from 1928 on
by an Intergovernmental Advisory Commission of
representatives of thirteen governments. Representatives of the High Commissioner in various cities
and countries carried on the work of relief and
settlement. The League bore the administrative
costs of the office of the High Commissioner, but
the relief and settlement work were chiefly financed
by philanthropic organizations, such as the American Red Cross, Near East Relief, Save the Children
Fund, Armenian (Lord Mayor's) Fund, etc.

In 1926 the High Commissioner obtained from a

Governmental Conference the agreement to institute a special stamp to be placed on the documents of travel and identity issued to those refugees who had the means of paying. The charge for the stamp was five gold francs, and the proceeds were placed in a revolving fund established by the League for the purpose of moving and settling refugees without means.

Dr. Nansen's responsibilities as outlined by the League Assembly were "to coordinate the action of governments and private organizations for the relief of Russian refugees, to regulate the legal status of a large class of persons who had been rendered stateless, and to assist them to find permanent homes and work."

Therefore, Dr. Nansen had to create an organization that coordinated the philanthropic activities of private, i.e. non-governmental agencies with international and governmental action. The High Commission was to be a kind of holding company for the existing voluntary agencies, and a bridge between the two elements, the governmental one and the private one.

WHAT NANSEN FACED

Because any future agency that handles refugee questions on a big scale will necessarily have to face the same technical problems, it is of more than historical interest to see whether, and if so how and to what degree, Dr. Nansen succeeded in his purpose.

The first refugees to be entrusted to Dr. Nansen's care were the 1,500,000 Russians who poured forth between 1918–24 as an immediate consequence of the Russian Revolution and Civil War. They were soon joined by 1,500,000 Greeks, who in 1922 were forced to leave their homes in Anatolia and the Turkish provinces as a result of the Graeco-Turkish war. Before long another category of refugees was added: 350,000 Armenians who fled from Asia Minor with the Greek populations.

The Russians and Armenians presented one group of problems, the Greeks another. While the former had no government to care for them and no country to receive them, the Greeks had both. A protocol attached to the Treaty of Lausanne provided for the exchange of Greek and Turkish populations. But neither the Greek Government alone nor the philanthropic organizations could tackle the huge task of repatriating a great number of people to a small country impoverished by ten years of warfare. Yet there was no time to lose; the refugees were herded in the ports of Greece, practically destitute. In his most instructive book, *I Was Sent to Athens*,

Mr. Henry Morgenthau, Sr. described the plight of the refugees as follows:

"The condition of these people upon their arrival in Greece was pitiable beyond description. They had been herded upon every kind of craft that could float, crowded so densely on board that in many cases they had only room to stand on deck. There they were exposed alternately to the blistering sun and cold rain of variable September and October. In one case, which I myself beheld, seven thousand people were packed into a vessel that would have been crowded with a load of two thousand. In this and many other cases there was neither food to eat nor water to drink, and in numerous instances the ships were buffeted about for several days at sea before their wretched human cargoes could be brought to land. Typhoid and smallpox swept through the ships. Lice infested everyone. Babies were born on board. Men and women went insane. Some leaped overboard to end their miseries in the sea. Those who survived were landed without shelter upon the open beach, loaded with filth, racked by fever, without blankets or even warm clothing, without food and without money.

"Besides these horrors the refugees endured every form of sorrow—the loss of husbands by wives, loss of wives by husbands, loss of children through death or straying, all manner of illnesses.

"If ever the Four Horsemen of the Apocalypse rode down upon a nation it was when this appalling host appeared upon the shores of Greece, that was trampled by the flying hoofs of their chargers and scourged by the spectral riders of War, Famine, Pestilence and Death."

AND WHAT NANSEN DID

The first step Dr. Nansen took was to use his office as a clearing house for the relief effort and to draw up, with the help of Sir Arthur Salter, a settlement plan based on a loan to the Greek Government. The complexity of the task made it necessary to set up a special commission, the Greek Refugee Settlement Commission, which was attached to the Finance and Economic Section of the League. This commission was first headed by Henry Morgenthau, Sr. of New York and then by the late Charles P. Howland of New York. British officers with experience of Indian settlement and two Greek members were appointed to it.

The Commission, established in September, 1923, was vested by the Greek Government with plenary powers to proceed with permanent agricultural and urban settlement of the refugees. Before that, in June, 1923, the Council of the League had recommended an international loan of £10,000,000 for this purpose. The League, under Sir Arthur Salter's financial advice, had successfully handled complicated financial problems in Austria and Hungary. Still, it was no easy job to get the Bank of England to float the loan. The Greeks had just thrown over the monarchy, and political chaos seemed around the corner. Nobody knew whether the Commission would have the ability to handle the settlement. The financial situation in Europe was not propitious for a loan. Moreover, in order to prevent starvation, the Commission needed a cash advance of £2,000,000 because the starving refugees could not wait until the bonds were sold. But Mr. Morgenthau eventually convinced Mr. Montagu Norman and Sir Otto Niemeyer that without any serious risk they could take part in the biggest philanthropic enterprise in history and, incidentally, stabilize the Balkans. Of the long-term loan, secured on certain revenues of the Greek Government, £2,500,000 were placed in Greece, the remainder, £7,500,000, in Great Britain and the United States.

IN MACEDONIA, TURKEY, AND GREECE

With the proceeds of this loan the Commission built urban settlements for about 600,000 people and established industries which gave them productive employment. For the rest they built over 1,500 villages in Macedonia and provided land, stock, tools, and seed. Room for these settlements was made by the removal of 375,000 Moslems to Turkey under the provision for the exchange of populations of the before-mentioned Protocol to the Treaty of Lausanne. Considering the fact that these refugees increased the existing population of Greece by 25 per cent and that two-thirds of them had been completely destitute, a miracle of inventiveness, altruistic energy and persistence had been accomplished by the Commission, and this in the short period of seven years. For the Commission was liquidated in December, 1930, turning the final completion of the settlement work over to the Greek Government.

A similar League Commission on behalf of the 120,000 Bulgarian refugees from Greece was set up under the League protocol of September 8th, 1926. Here, too, the settlement was financed by an international loan. Here, too, the Commission completed its work, which was of course on a much smaller scale, in the short period of six years, the Commission winding up early in 1932.

Obviously, the fact that the Greek and Bulgarian refugees had countries willing to receive them made the solution of their problem comparatively easy. Still, the absorption of a big body of mostly destitute refugees by an impoverished country in so short a period was made possible only by the cooperation of government, private initiative, and the League of Nations.

The refugees, incidentally, proved in a relatively short time to be a blessing to Greece. They increased the production of cereals, tobacco and silk. They planted vines, introduced the cultivation of high-class Sultana raisins, and started the carpet industry. This goes to show how the perfect coordination of the necessary forces can bring about a constructive solution of the refugee problem!

FOR RUSSIANS AND ARMENIANS

The action on behalf of Russian and Armenian refugees was fundamentally different. Here were literally men without a country. Most of the Russian refugees sat at first in the countries bordering Russia—merely waiting in the hope that the Soviet regime might blow up and that they could then go back. But this hope did not materialize. Nor did another hope materialize—that a great part of them might be repatriated. Between 1922–24, out of a million and a half people, only 13,000 were taken back by the Soviet regime with full amnesty, and it had by then become evident that not many more could safely be returned.

Dr. Nansen was faced with the task of arranging permanent settlement not only for these 1,500,-000 Russian refugees, but also for 350,000 Armenians who, at the time of the Greeks' expulsion from Anatolia, had fled into Greece, Bulgaria and Syria.

The Armenians are refugees *sui generis*. They had had forty years of massacres under Ottoman rule behind them when the World War started. The outbreak of war was a signal for the Young Turks to pursue their policy of extermination with a carefully planned ruthlessness unparalleled in history. The news of these atrocities came as a real shock to the Allies, who had promised the Armenian people freedom and independence, provided their men joined the Entente armies. And really, of the quarter of a million of those who escaped the slaughter, many joined the Allied Armies and fell for the Allied cause.

That is why when Turkey was beaten at the end of the war, Allied statesmen vied with one another in professions of indebtedness to the Armenians.

But in order to set up an independent Armenia, as had been promised, the occupation of Turkish-Armenia by Allied troups was indispensable. This seemed, to the grateful Allied statesmen, too much of a sacrifice. The Turks remained masters over Turkish-Armenia and the cause of the Armenians was betrayed. With the rebirth of Turkey under Mustapha Kemal all hope of settling the Armenians within the former body of Turkey vanished.

THE NANSEN PASSPORT

In the case of Russians and Armenians alike, Dr. Nansen had to deal with people without protection from any government. His first task was therefore to regulate their legal status and to give them some sort of identity paper. For this purpose he created in 1922 the "Nansen certificate" which was adopted by fifty governments. The Nansen certificate was valid for one year only and issuance was discretionary with individual governments.

Inasmuch as it was not valid for return to the country of issue unless specifically inscribed to that effect, the Nansen certificate was—at least as a travel passport—inferior to national passports, some countries being reluctant about letting people in who could not go back where they came from. A convention in 1933, however, provided that the Nansen passport should authorize the return of its holder to the country of issue and that it could be extended for a period of six months. Though only five nations—Bulgaria, Czechoslovakia, Denmark, Italy and Norway—actually ratified this convention, and three others—Belgium, France and Egypt —signed it, the Convention is practically in force. In an emergency, moreover, the Nansen certificate proved its value: namely, when in 1933 the Russian-Jewish refugees in Germany were compelled to flee once more—this time before the Nazi revolution—they found that their Nansen certificates opened the frontiers for them.

THE MAN ATTACHED TO A PAPER

It is a fantastic commentary on the inhumanity of our times that for thousands and thousands of people a piece of paper with a stamp on it is the difference between life and death, and that scores of people have blown their brains out because they could not get it. But there is no doubt that, by and large, the Nansen certificate is the greatest thing that has happened for the individual refugee. It returned to him his lost identity. The refugee could never be sure whether he would get a labor permit by means of the Nansen certificate, but he could be sure that *without* the Nansen certificate he would *never* get it.

Moreover, the Nansen certificate gave him moral

protection. While the refugee without an identification paper was exposed to petty police tyrannies, the holders of the Nansen passport could turn to the representatives of the High Commission in various capitals, who afforded them a kind of consular service. These Commissioners took matters up with the ministries when expulsion orders were issued, or labor permits refused, and in a more general way saw to it that the governments kept the arrangements they had entered into on behalf of the refugees. All this together meant a big step forward toward the solution of the individual refugee problem.

The Nansen certificate was extended to Chaldean, Assyrian and Turkish refugees, and in 1935 to the refugees from the Saar, who were all under the protection of the League; but it never reached the political *sans patries* from Hungary, Italy and Spain who were not considered as coming within the League's province.

Concerning these stateless persons outside of League protection, the Connection and Transit Organization of the League adopted at its third conference in 1927 a series of recommendations to the governments to employ a uniform document of identity and travel, similar to the Nansen certificate but bearing the mention "good for return."

These recommendations were accepted in principle by most states, and the "international passport" came to life.

The years following the end of the War were on the whole good years for Dr. Nansen's work. In these years he not only succeeded in regulating the legal status for the refugees, but he was able, also, to find work for them in various countries. I have already said that during these years the refugees had a definite place in the labor market—namely, to fill the gaps left by those who had been killed in the War. France, for instance, offered to place all refugees who were able to work, and by 1925 had received 400,000 Russians and 63,000 Armenians. Some 135,000 Russians went to China and 75,000 were established in Germany.

THE LATE ALBERT THOMAS, AND
HIS PLANS

In 1924 the Council decided that the High Commissioner should surrender a part of his responsibilities—namely, the task of finding productive employment for refugees—to the International Labor Organization, thus retaining only responsibility for the legal and political side of the problem. This decision was passed by the Assembly on September

25th, 1924, and adopted by the Governing Body of the ILO in October, 1924. The liaison between the High Commission and the ILO was effected in the person of the Assistant High Commissioner who was at the same time Chief of Section for Refugee Questions at the ILO.

The Director of the ILO was the late French socialist, Albert Thomas, a man of great heart and fiery imagination. Thomas understood as well as Dr. Nansen that the refugee problem would not be confined to the already existing categories of refugees. Certain countries, so he figured—especially Italy, Poland and Turkey—suffered from an actual surplus of population which eventually would have to flow off. Both thought that this efflux of surplus populations was inevitable if a future war were to be avoided. And in cooperation with Dr. Nansen Thomas started to work at a plan to intercept and direct the actual and expected stream of migration.

The essence of this plan was that settlements should be organized in the form of agricultural communities, the basic unit of which was to be a kind of synthetic settlement family—the gist of the matter being that the ballast of the old and sick, which the natural family has to drag along, should be counter-balanced for settlement purpose by an addition of assorted young people.

Both Dr. Nansen and Albert Thomas understood that European agricultural settlers would have to be assured of a certain measure of comfort beyond that available to native settlers, otherwise they would move to the big cities at the first opportunity. Therefore, sufficient funds had to be raised. According to their scheme, the work of settlement was to be financed by both the emigration and the immigration countries, together with the League of Nations.

The League under this scheme would float a loan, part of which the country of origin would accept as payment for the emigrants' passage and for the farm machinery which he would take along, and which the immigrant countries would agree to admit without duty. With the other part of the loan the settler would pay for his new land and house, animals and seed, and for provisions to see him through until after the first harvest.

The increased value of the cultivated soil, the creation of electric power, etc., would make the loan profitable for the new country. To the emigration country, acceptance of the bonds would be made profitable by giving occupation to transportation companies and industries and by creating new outlets for exports.

The League was to guarantee the interest on the loan, and the settler would start payment of interest three years after the first harvest. The loan was to be amortized in twenty years.

The first settlement experiments along these lines were to have been made with the Russian and Armenian refugees. Unfortunately, they never got beyond the stage of study. Thus—following the 1924 Assembly recommendation—a Commission of Enquiry, headed by Dr. Nansen, was sent to study the possibilities of settlement in the region of Eriwan where large numbers of Armenians were already established. The Commission presented its report to the Assembly in 1925, proposing a loan of 9,000,000 roubles for settlement. A delegation appointed by Dr. Nansen visited South America in 1926 and reported that there were vast opportunities for the transfer of large groups to South American countries anxious to extend their program of immigration. An Intergovernmental Conference called by the High Commissioner in June, 1927, considered proposals received by the ILO from Argentina, Brazil and other states for settlement of 30,000 refugees. But the sums granted to the High Commission were so negligible that these large-scale plans were nipped in the bud.

MENNONITES TO PARAGUAY AND LUTHERANS TO BRAZIL

To be sure, various settlements were attempted in the following years. Thus, some thousands of Mennonites, who had been stranded in Eastern Siberia, were placed in Paraguay, and some thousands of Lutheran Russians in Brazil.

But except for the settlement of 28,000 Armenians in Syria under a plan administered by Mr. Ponsot, High Commissioner for France in Syria, and for which 2,500,000 French francs were advanced to the settlers, all these settlement experiments lacked the necessary financial foundation.

Unfortunately an insufficiently planned and financed settlement is worse than no settlement at all. An example is the attempted settlement of a thousand Russian gas-workers in South America—an experiment that was financed by the German Republic, which wished to get rid of some of its Russian refugees. This settlement was so insufficiently prepared and financed that five hundred of the thousand gas-workers came back to Germany within a year, some of them as coal-workers on freighters and some even as stowaways.

Dr. Nansen had started out as a strong believer in League of Nations principles. He believed that a problem like that of the refugee, which concerned the whole civilized world, should be attacked by collective effort, and he believed that it stood a reasonable chance of being solved by such effort.

But soon he found that the lofty ideals of cooperation had more reality in the League Covenant than in the hearts of its members. In this connection, the treatment of the Armenians by the Allied statesmen who had promised them so much was the source of his great grief. In one instance, the failure of the English to back his settlement plans in the Eriwan region drew tears of anger and an expression of bitter disappointment from him.

"In despair one can ask what it all meant! Was it, in reality, nothing but a gesture? Were they empty words with no serious intentions behind them?

"And the League of Nations! Has it no sense of responsibility either? By compelling its High Commissioner for Refugees, in spite of his repeated refusals, to take up the cause of the Armenian refugees, the League has almost certainly prevented others from organizing effective measures to help the Armenians. For it was assumed that the League of Nations would not espouse a cause of this nature without being able to deal with it satisfactorily—especially after all the pledges given by the powers. Does the League consider that it has done its duty? And does it imagine that it can let the matter drop without undermining the prestige of the League, especially in the East? . . .

"Woe to the Armenians that they were ever drawn into European politics! It would have been better for them, if the name of Armenia had never been uttered by any European diplomat. . . ."

This (taken from *Armenia and the Near East*) was his swan song.

THE DEATHS OF NANSEN AND THOMAS

Dr. Nansen died in May, 1930. To the world he was the savior of the refugee. He, himself, had no illusions about his work. He feared that what seemed like a permanent absorption of the refugees would turn out to be a temporary one, and he lived long enough to see the disastrous effect of the economic crisis on the lot of refugees all over the world.

Albert Thomas, whose soaring imagination had pictured hundreds of thousands of happy settlers building up a new civilization in South America, died two years later, in May, 1932.

After the deaths of these two men, all thought of large-scale settlement was abandoned. It was not only due to the fact that the economic crisis was unpropitious for ideas which involved far-seeing plans, international cooperation and great funds; it was much more serious that there were no outstanding personalities to take an interest in these ideas—personalities of warmth and generosity, of expert knowledge and energy, who would put their all into realizing such plans. Yet if the success of a plan depends on the cooperation of various agencies and governments, as is the case with mass settlement, nothing much can be done without powerful leadership.

THE LEAGUE AFTER NANSEN

In September, 1930, after the death of Dr. Nansen, the Assembly set up the Nansen International Office, an autonomous agency responsible to the League as successor to the High Commissioner. The Governing Body of the new-formed agency was composed of the Secretary General of the League, the Director of the ILO, four members appointed by the Intergovernmental Advisory Commission, three members appointed by the Advisory Committee of Relief Organizations and two representatives of relief organizations appointed by the Governing Body itself.

In 1929, shortly before the world depression set

in, the League Council and Assembly had decided
that the refugee problem was well on the way to
solution and that the office of High Commissioner
should be liquidated within ten years. The Nansen Office, in its new form, was to carry on and
liquidate the work within the prescribed period.

THE GROWTH OF DEFEATISM

From 1928 onward a new and alarming element
entered into the refugee problem—namely the depression and the unemployment resulting from it.
This hardened the hearts of people all over the
world toward refugees.

In almost all countries, labor legislation was
tightened up in order to secure preferential treatment for native labor as against that of immigrants,
and even where actual legislation was not passed,
trade union policies enforced preferential treatment. In all countries the depression stimulated the
so-called national spirit and encouraged the search
for a scapegoat to hold responsible for unsolved
economic difficulties. And the net effect was increased hostility to foreigners, and above all to
refugees.

Thus, unemployment hit the refugees harder
and affected them more disastrously than it did any
other group. At times, in some countries, fifty per

cent of all refugees were unemployed. And in countries where state-supported relief activities existed there were, and still are, strong movements to have all persons not yet citizens removed from the relief rolls.

Many governments thought it justifiable to rid themselves entirely of refugees. They refused to extend their permits to work, and served notice on them to quit the country as soon as their certificates of identity expired.

THE MAN WITHOUT A COUNTRY

Almost all countries tried to bar new immigration. It became a common experience for a refugee to find himself on a frontier, trapped between a country that had spat him out and a country that would not let him in. In that predicament he was practically forced to disobey the orders of one government or the other, by making an illicit entry and illicitly taking work. In 1935, in France alone, 4,000 Russian refugees were said to have expulsion orders standing against them. As they had committed the crime of taking work, contrary to orders, most of them were in jail—thus burdening the French Treasury considerably. A case is on record where a single refugee cost the French Government about 29,000 francs. The total cost of maintain-

ing the refugees who are in French prisons is estimated at 12,000,000 francs for the years 1935 and
1936—an extremely cruel and excessively senseless
method of dealing with the refugee problem.

To mitigate cases of such cruel hardship among
refugees was the immediate task of the Nansen Office. As early as 1928 Dr. Nansen had called a conference of the representatives of governments and
made certain recommendations to them, aimed to
waive rules restricting the employment of foreign
labor and particularly urging the states not to expel
refugees from their countries until they were certain
that they would be received in another country.

Though these recommendations have been repeated in annual resolutions of the League Assembly,
most of the governments have not felt bound by
them. The Convention drafted by the Intergovernmental Advisory Commission for Refugees in 1933,
which was meant to make the above recommendations more effective, has been ratified to date by
only five governments—Bulgaria, Czechoslovakia,
Norway, Denmark and Italy. Lately, the French
Chamber and Senate have voted a law authorizing
France's participation in the Convention, and the
Belgian Government has submitted to Parliament a
draft law of ratification.

But even the governments accepting the Convention made reservations, as regards the right of refugees to work. Moreover, the Convention makes provision only for the Russian and Armenian refugees—the so-called Nansen refugees—and to a certain extent for the German refugees.

Though the Intergovernmental Advisory Commission, which drafted the Convention of 1933, recommended that the Council reconsider the question of extending these arrangements to all categories of exiles, the Council in May, 1934, decided that such a step would be inopportune. A Committee of Experts, appointed by the League Council in 1931 to study the question of assistance to indigent foreigners generally, was still less successful; in 1933, when a Draft Convention was drawn up in Geneva, the experts of Denmark, Switzerland and the United States doubted the willingness of their countries to enter into any international convention providing for assistance to indigent foreigners. The Committee made only a recommendation to the effect "that the participation of foreigners in the benefits of unemployment insurance and various forms of assistance to unemployed should be regulated as early as possible and in the most liberal manner by means of an ILO Convention on the basis of the principle of equality treatment."

However, the attempt of the International Labor Conference of 1934 to obtain agreement on such a convention failed.

As few of the governments acted upon them, all these conventions, agreements and recommendations were of no earthly use. The fact remained that the refugees were and are the foremost victims of unemployment—not only because it is inevitable that when workmen have to be dismissed the alien is dismissed first, but also because the refugees' problem of unemployment is further aggravated by government action. Relief measures are not generally applied to aliens. Many states have enacted legislation which prohibits the employer from engaging foreign workmen save in very restricted measure. Many countries do their best to get rid of unemployed aliens altogether.

Thus, after the refugee had gone through the hardships and heartbreak of flight from his country, he was thrown back into still more hopeless insecurity. As this writer heard one of them remark in despair, "A man can pull through such disaster once, but he can not pull through it twice."

THE NEW WAVES OF MIGRATION

This was the situation when suddenly, unexpectedly, the stream of migration broke loose again. In 1932 it seized 25,000 Assyrians and threw them out of Iraq. Then, from 1933 onward, it began sweeping tens of thousands of Germans out of Germany.

It would take too much space to tell the whole painful story of the Assyrians in the last fifty years. Only this: like the Armenians, they had been badly treated by the Turkish Government and consequently they entered the World War on the side of the Allies, declaring war against Turkey in 1915. The Turks invaded their territory and burnt their villages, and the Assyrians had to flee. When the War was over, the grateful Allied statesmen talked about establishing an independent Assyrian kingdom, but as little came of it as of the independent Armenian state.

The only chance for the Assyrians was to settle in the new kingdom of Iraq. This kingdom was placed under a British mandate where it was meant to remain for at least twenty-five years. But in 1932 the British Government thought Iraq sufficiently developed to stand on its own feet and recommended it for membership in the League of Nations.

When in the Mandate Commission of the League some apprehension was voiced about the Iraq Government's spirit of tolerance toward religious and racial minorities, the British High Commissioner assured the Commission that the Iraquis' spirit of tolerance was above suspicion. The British mandate was brought to an end, and the Iraquis—to make a long story short—celebrated their new independence with a massacre of the Assyrians. Many of them were killed and their villages looted, and it became clear that they could not hold out in Iraq any longer. They took refuge near Mosul, where a great refugee camp was set up for them until the Nansen Office settled most of them in Syria.

AND, FINALLY, THE GERMANS

The last to be caught up by the stream of migration are the Germans, who fled from their country after the Nazis had come to power in 1933, and the Austrians who began fleeing from their country when it was swallowed by Hitler in March, 1938. Statistics show that there were 150,000 German refugees by the end of 1937, but they are increasing steadily, and they may be more than 175,-000 by now. As for the Austrians, no figures are available yet; but so much is sure, at least 200,000 will have to leave their country or starve.

Anyway, statistics mean little for a group of exiles which can pride itself on scientists like Albert Einstein and James Franck; or novelists like Thomas Mann, Heinrich Mann, Eric Maria Remarque, Arnold Zweig, Annette Kolbe—to name only a few; or a theatrical producer like Max Reinhardt; or actors like Elisabeth Bergner and Fritz Kortner; or musicians like Fritz Klemperer, Bruno Walter and Arthur Schnabel; or painters, such as Oscar Kokoschka; or playwrights, like Bert Brecht or Karl Zuckmayer; or physicians like Schick, the inventor of the Schick test for diphtheria.

Practically everybody who in world opinion had stood for what was currently called German culture prior to 1933 is already a refugee—the number greatly augmented since the conquest of Austria, and including many who fled first to Vienna from Germany, and now must flee again.

The German and Austrian refugees are divided into two separate groups: Non-Aryans who were obliged to leave their homeland as a result of legislative measures against them and "political undesirables"—who had to leave their country for political reasons.

The question of aid for refugees from Germany was brought first before the League of Nations at the annual International Labor Conference in 1933, when the ILO was asked to take measures for their relief and settlement. Then at the League Assembly the Netherlands delegation urged that the set-

tlement of refugees, who had been admitted into
countries adjacent to Germany, should be regarded
as "an economic, financial and social problem
which can be solved only by international collaboration."

The Second Commission of the Assembly
adopted a resolution which asked the Council to
nominate a High Commissioner "to negotiate and
direct the international collaboration and particularly to provide, as far as possible, work for the
refugees in countries which are able to offer it."

At this time, Germany was still a member of the
League, and the German delegation opposed the
proposal that the High Commissioner should be
directly attached to the League.

To spare embarrassment to Germany the "High
Commissioner for Refugees coming from Germany" was set up as an entirely autonomous organization. The Council appointed an American,
Mr. James G. McDonald, as the High Commissioner, and invited fifteen states to send representatives to the Governing Body. Of those, all but three
accepted the invitation—among them all the countries adjacent to Germany except Austria: also Great
Britain, Italy, Jugoslavia, Sweden, the United
States, and Uruguay.

Spain, Argentina and Brazil declined.

The organization of the High Commission for German refugees was similar to that of the Nansen Office. Besides the Governing Body of the thirteen governmental representatives, there was an Advisory Council composed of representatives of philanthropic organizations. The seat of the office was first at Lausanne, but in October, 1934, it was removed to London, thus expressing geographically the complete detachment of the High Commissioner from the League. This complete detachment was expressed also in other ways: While the League carried the administrative costs of the Nansen Office, the expenses of the High Commissioner's office were borne entirely by contributions from philanthropic organizations, save for a contribution made by the Swedish Government. The reports of the High Commissioner, moreover, were not submitted to the League Council, as were those of the Nansen Office.

The first meeting of the Governing Body in Lausanne in December, 1933, defined the scope of the activity of the High Commissioner as one

"to stimulate the fund-raising activities of the philanthropic bodies, and to coordinate the efforts of the organization in many countries for the settlement, the emigration and the re-training

of the refugees, and to negotiate with governments both on technical questions such as passports and on the admission of groups of refugees
into countries where there is opportunity for
their absorption."

One of the first tasks of the High Commissioner
was to have the international passport of 1927 extended to the refugees who were still Germans, but
could not obtain a renewal of their German passports, nor a new German document. To this the
governments generally agreed.

Then the Governing Body of the High Commission made recommendations to the represented
states concerning the maintenance of permits of
residence and permits of work in favor of the German refugees.

But, as in measures affecting other categories of
refugees, these recommendations were of little effect. Things were still more complicated by the fact
that the relations between the High Commission
and the various governments were entirely based on
persuasion and consultation and lacked the moral
authority which the Nansen Office at least theoretically enjoyed by means of invoking the resolutions
of the League Assembly—although this had lately
not proved very effective either.

The German refugees had to cope with the consequences of the economic crisis. Of course, the distinguished scientists, scholars, men of letters, musicians and artists among them were everywhere welcomed as assets. Of 650 professors who were dismissed from German universities it was possible to place 600 in either temporary or permanent positions where they could go on with their scientific work. For this task alone £300,000 was subscribed, largely by members of British and American universities and American research foundations.

An institution like the "University in Exile" which the initiative of the scholar and humanitarian, Professor Alvin Johnson, called into existence in New York City, has developed in the four years of its existence into an important outpost of free science.

But, of course, only an elite was thus easily placed. An exceptionally high number of German refugees belong to the professional class, the balance being small tradesmen and clerks. Very few had ever been employed in agriculture or in manual work. In spite of these difficulties, a comparatively large number of them found refuge in a surprisingly short time. This is explained by the fact that wealthier refugees succeeded in getting out at least that part of their fortunes which was left when a 25 per cent flight tax and the loss on the sale of blocked marks were deducted.

PHILANTHROPY HAS BEEN GENEROUS

Moreover, various philanthropic organizations have put funds at their disposal, which amount by now to around £3,000,000.

The distribution of the funds is carried out by the private organizations, while the High Commissioner makes only recommendations as to allocation of the money. Thus 20,000 refugees were repatriated in the countries of Eastern Europe, 20,000 found at least temporary refuge in France, about 35,000 came to the United States, 4,000 to England, 7,500 were absorbed in the Netherlands, Sweden and Belgium, 5,000 in Switzerland, Italy, Czechoslovakia and Jugoslavia, 3,000 went to South Africa, 7,500 to Brazil, 5,000 to Argentina and 4,000 to other South American and Central American countries. The greatest number of them, 42,000, were settled in Palestine.

GERMAN REFUGEES AND PALESTINE

The Jewish Agency for Palestine, a body recognized by the Mandatory Government as representative of the Jewish organizations, created a special bureau for the settlement of German Jews in Palestine. This bureau placed a large number of German Jews in agricultural and industrial work. Others who came in as "capitalists"—as such they had to show at least one thousand pounds—have made their own way to Palestine.

It is highly interesting and significant that the settlement of German Jews in Palestine was only to the smallest extent—about £1,000,000—financed by Jewish charity. The far greater part of the settlement of German Jews in Palestine was made financially possible by means of a trade-and-transfer arrangement between the Nazi Government and the Haavara, an organization for the transfer of capital of German-Jewish emigrants. This arrangement is important and suggestive.

Under it, the German exporter takes marks out of the Haavara fund in payment for German goods exported to Palestine. These Haavara marks are earmarked emigrant funds. The equivalent of these marks is credited to the immigrants in Palestine. By this method about 82,000,000 marks in merchandise have been transferred to Palestine in the last five years. Thus 14,000 refugee families have been settled, who otherwise could not have entered Palestine because, at the rate of the blocked mark, they could not have raised the thousand pounds.

This has proved to be the only realistic approach to a financial solution of the German refugee problem so far.

This work of settlement, however, was almost entirely restricted to Jewish refugees.

In 1935 the High Commissioner, assisted by Dr. S. G. Inman, made a visit to the principal countries in South America, with the purpose of finding openings for settlements of groups of refugees, both Jewish and non-Jewish. This visit had no results.

The growing difficulty of securing homes for the refugees and the tightening of the measures driving Non-Aryans out of professional life in Germany made it increasingly necessary that the League should consider the question of refugees as a whole, that the various organizations concerned with refugee questions should be amalgamated into one organ which should be an integral part of the League. Lord Cecil of Chelwood, chairman of the Governing Body of the High Commissioner for Refugees coming from Germany, taking this idea up before the British House of Lords in February, 1935, pointed out that such an organ would be subject to the whole mechanism of the League, would allow Assembly and Council to debate any matters which came up, and public opinion to keep track of everything that was going on.

MCDONALD'S RESIGNATION

The seriousness of the German refugee problem was revealed to the world at large by the publication of the letter of resignation of Mr. McDonald as High Commissioner to the Secretary General of the League. In this letter, which is an admirable humanitarian document, Mr. McDonald declared that the care and settlement of the refugees could be borne by the already heavily burdened private organizations only if the further increase of refugees would be checked. To do this, Mr. McDonald pointed out, would be a job for the League of Nations.

"The moral authority of the League of Nations and of State Members of the League must be directed toward a determined appeal to the German Government in the name of humanity and of the principles of the public law of Europe. . . . The growing sufferings of the persecuted minority in Germany and the menace of the growing exodus call for friendly but firm intercession with the German Government, by all pacific means, on the part of the League of Nations, of its Member States and other members of the community of nations."

If the League made any effort along the suggested lines, it was never known to the public—nor had it any effect on Nazi policies. Nevertheless, when the question of refugees came up in the Assembly of 1936, a resolution was adopted indicating that although the previous decision as to the closing of the Nansen Office and of the office of the High Commissioner should continue effective, the League had not lost interest in the problem. The resolution recommended that in 1938 at the latest the whole refugee problem should be examined and that general principles should be adopted for the League's future action.

For two years the fate of the League's refugee organizations hung in the balance. The prolongation of the Nansen Office was consistently fought by Soviet Russia because it looks after the interests of White Russians who are considered enemies of the Soviet state. Italy, too, showed a certain hostility toward the Nansen Office. Just when the growing impact of the refugee problem made the existence of a competent refugee agency more necessary than ever, it had to fear that the League would disclaim further responsibility for the protection of these unfortunate people.

This fear, however, did not wholly come true.

And, in any case, the past efforts of the League

on behalf of the refugees have been only partly successful. Lack of funds and cooperation thwarted the large-scale plans of settlement advocated by two men of imagination: Nansen and Albert Thomas.

The League was never able to dam the stream of migration at the source—or even to limit it to any extent.

Nevertheless, such improvements in the position of refugees as have been apparent in the last seventeen years were directly effected by Dr. Nansen and through him by the League. The League afforded to the refugees a measure of political and judicial protection, without which they would have been entirely defenseless and without hope. Nor must we forget the successful settlement of Greeks and Bulgarians, in which the League had the leadership. For here the League, though sometimes weak in energy and poor in vision, accomplished a humanitarian deed which justifies its whole existence.

CHAPTER THREE

The Jewish Refugees

WHEN THE EXODUS from Germany started in 1933, the world began to look at the refugee problem as exclusively Jewish.

This is an error. The refugee question is not even essentially Jewish in those countries which make anti-Semitism their leading idea! Many of the German refugees are as "Nordic" as can be, but have had to flee for political reasons, because they were liberals, socialists, democrats, pacifists, or religious devotees. As for the new stream of exiles from former Austria, it includes monarchists of aristocratic background, former members of Chancellor Schuschnigg's Fatherland Front, and Catholics.

WHO IS A JEW?

And among those who were obliged to leave their homeland as a result of legislative measures enacted against them—the so-called Aryan laws—only a fraction are Jews by the standards of any other world than that of Mr. Hitler. Many of them

56

are members of the Catholic and Protestant churches; numbers are largely assimilated racially and most of them are wholly assimilated culturally. But though they think of themselves as Christians —possibly for generations back—and are as German in their social and cultural traits as anyone can be, they are discriminated against in Germany as "Non-Aryans."

So far there has been no census of Non-Aryans in Germany. The 1933 figure of 550,000 German Jews covers only the recorded 100 per cent Jews of the Jewish community. It does not even cover the racially 100 per cent Jews who are baptized, nor, it goes without saying, persons who have 75 per cent, 50 per cent, 25 per cent or 12½ per cent Jewish blood. These Non-Aryans are estimated at between one and a half and three millions. Among them are many German aristocrats and the flower of the German bourgeoisie. The reason for this gap between minimum and maximum estimates is largely that the exact point where Aryanism ends and Non-Aryanism begins has not yet been established.

Up to now, Aryanism has been determined not so much by law as by party decisions and by circumstances. Thus, a publisher must prove his Aryan descent way back to the year 1800—that is, to his great-grandparents—whereas a journalist has to prove only that his grandparents were Aryans. In other words, the Aryan laws are still fluid. The radical wing of the Nazi Party is all for a general extension of the *Ahnenbeweis* (ancestor proof) back to 1800; and it now seems that this will be done.

According to the present Aryan laws, the 50 per cent Jews enjoy certain advantages compared to the 100 per cent Jews. But these advantages are merely on paper. For instance, the law does not forbid marriages between 50 per cent Jews and Aryans, provided the government gives permission; but no case is known where such permission has been granted. Both full-blooded and half-blooded Jews are excluded from schools and universities, from the labor front and from the Reichs-organizations, membership in which is obligatory for all who wish to practise a trade or profession. In education and professional life the half-Jew is almost as badly off as the full-blooded Jew.

It is different with the 25 per cent Jew. Theoretically he has the choice between "passing" by marrying an Aryan or becoming Jewish by marrying a Jew. But actually either is difficult. The writer knows of a case of two 25 per cent Jewish daughters of a great scientist: the government withheld permission from one to marry her Nazi fiancé, from the other to marry her Jewish fiancé.

The 25 per cent Jew cannot hold a government post or become an officer; on the other hand, in economic life he is, up to now, as good as an Aryan. But even this can be changed from one day to the next by party decision. *Therefore, the Aryan laws affect one to three million people in Germany who are not Jews* except by a fantastic stretch of imagination.

It has been estimated that the application of the Aryan laws in Austria will affect not only the 200,000 members of the Jewish Community, but 800,000 Non-Aryans—nearly one million persons, one-sixth of the Austrian population—whose livelihood will be in danger.

Nevertheless, since 750,000 Jews are the foremost victims of persecution in Germany and former Austria; since anti-Semitic propaganda already casts a shadow over the lives of nearly two millions in Hungary, and Rumania; since the problem of three and a half million Polish Jews was acute long before Mr. Hitler thought up his Aryan ideology; since thus the number of Jewish refugees within the immediate future will possibly be augmented—it would be ostrichism to close one's eyes to the fact that the question of the Jewish refugee is a major question of international politics.

The challenge is one which the Jews of the

whole world must face—and above all the Jews of America, who constitute one-fourth of world Jewry. It is a challenge, moreover, to the pre-science and common sense of any racial or religious minority which has ever known persecution or discrimination anywhere in the past; for if these do not now protest the abuse of other minorities what moral grounds will they have for protesting if once again their own rights are threatened?

But it is—even more importantly—a challenge to all responsible political circles, not only to those who condemn persecution for humanitarian reasons but also to those who, taking a purely practical view, fear that starving minorities within the anti-Semitic countries, and an uncontrolled flow of wandering Jews outside, will add further elements of unrest to an already restless world. Nor can the anti-Semitic governments themselves be indifferent, for in the long run—though they may find it gratifying to have the Jews "liquidated"—it is uncomfortable to have in one's midst a body of desperate pariahs.

THE REACTION OF WORLD JEWRY

Up to now, neither the democratic governments, nor the creators of the problem have made an attempt to achieve a constructive solution.

The German Government looks on while a problem is growing up for which mass starvation seems hardly a solution, even for Germany!

Responsible political circles in the world find it too ticklish a problem to tackle because it may imply interference in the internal affairs of other countries, and also because they are afraid that to raise the question of emigration may produce anti-Semitism in their own countries.

As for the Jews of the world, they have made a few gestures of understandable but ineffective protest against Nazi Germany—the boycott the strongest. But the boycott did not substantially weaken the Nazis economically and in any case did not soften their anti-Semitic policy. Instead, the boycott acted as a boomerang against the boycotting Jews in the democratic countries, by awakening anti-Semitism among non-Jews who wanted to do business with Germany, Nazi or not.

In addition, the Jews practised a magnificently generous philanthropy. They placed huge sums at the disposal of the Jewish organizations which were helping numbers of German Jews to get out of Germany and to find a refuge elsewhere, temporary or permanent. Yet, as anti-Semitic policies spread through Europe it becomes clearer and clearer that charity is not enough. It cannot be too often emphasized that the problem must be regarded and treated as one of international politics. The only approach to a solution must be a political approach.

THE UNIQUE NATURE OF TODAY'S ANTI-SEMITISM

There have been anti-Semitic movements in the world before. Russian pogroms under the Tsar are alive in the memories of many. But the Jewish persecution of our era is peculiar. It is not directed against the ghetto Jew alone, but against the Jewish race as such—against the Jew who has retained his religion and against the Jew who has discarded it.

Moreover a Jewish race is actually created by fiat, disregarding most of the scientific opinion of the world. Even the Nazi anthropologist Gunther admits the existence of Jews who have all the racial characteristics of "Nordics," "Alpines," "Mediterraneans" or "Balts." And the Nuremberg laws have even a fundamental lack of logic. For they admit that there is a point in inter-breeding where a Jew ceases to be a Jew. They admit the possibility of complete racial absorption, and therefore logic should lead them to solve their problem—if they consider they have one—by racial absorption.

But this artificial creation of a race problem within the white race puts the Jews in a madly impossible position.

Throughout the Middle Ages and until the Russian pogroms of the nineteenth century, the Jews, when persecution overtook them, were in the ghetto. There they lived, wrapped up in themselves, firmly entrenched in a civilization of their own—a religious civilization. When an acquisitive prince, a fanatic priest, a malcontent mob decided to take the money of the Jews, to punish them as heretics, to ransack their homes, they still had a refuge in their very Jewishness. The religion based on the Old Testament was a living force. Even when wandering the earth, they still enjoyed their own civilization—the worship of their God. Wherever ten male Jews gathered, there was the temple.

The assimilated German and Austrian Jews outlawed by Hitler have no separate civilization of their own to fall back on. The doors of the ghetto were opened one hundred and twenty-five years ago. Formal religion, if these assimilated Jews practise it at all, plays in their lives the subdued role it plays in the lives of most of their Christian contemporaries. Religion is no longer their civilization. They had felt so little Jewish that they had lost all sense of danger. To be sure, Dr. Adolf Stoecker in Berlin and Georg von Schoenerer in Vienna did their level best to stir up anti-Semitism in the eighties. The *Affaire* Dreyfus brought along a wave of anti-Semitism in the nineties. But these movements were limited. While they did not die down altogether, they were neither officially adopted by governments nor backed by the upper classes.

While Jews could not become officers in the German Army and rarely could hold government posts under the monarchy, the Kaiser himself had personal friends among Jewish industrialists and bankers, and marriages between German and Austrian aristocrats and the daughters of wealthy Jews were favored by the court from the beginning of the nineteenth century.

The German and Austrian Jews are Germans and Austrians. The only civilization they know is the civilization they shared with the German and Austrian nations. When Hitler's laws denied them this civilization, they found themselves in a moral and cultural void. And there was no way out. The aristocrat of the French Revolution could save himself by becoming a *citoyen*. The Russian bourgeois could save himself by becoming a *tovaritsch*. The German Jew can never become an Aryan.

REPERCUSSIONS IN CENTRAL EUROPE

Though German Aryanism will not get Mr. Hitler very far in the Eastern European countries (as their peoples are not "Nordic" at all, but are Slavs, Magyars, or of mixed races), it is to be feared that a Nazified Hungary, or an even partly Nazified Czechoslovakia, would eventually deal with their highly assimilated Jews according to Hitler's principles.

There are 400,000 Jews in Hungary, forming 5.1 per cent of the population. 8.7 per cent of them are in the professions and public services, 75 per cent in trade, industry and finance. Until now they have played a leading role in banking, in the textile industry and in the export business. They have also distinguished themselves as scientists, physicians and lawyers—and they especially excel as playwrights and composers of musical comedies.

A strong anti-Semitic feeling was latent in Hungary as a result of the Communist revolution, which counted among its leaders several Jews—and it has increased during the last years by force of violent Nazi propaganda. Recently a bill was voted limiting the proportion of Jews—and Christians baptized after 1919, i.e. after the Communist revolution—in industry, trade and the professions to 20 per cent.

The Hungarian Premier, Bela Imredy, introduced this bill as a means to curb the Hungarian Nazis by making concessions to their prejudices. To what degree it will affect the material situation of the Hungarian Jews cannot be ascertained yet. Nor can it be foreseen whether the matter will rest there —or whether this is only a beginning of measures driving the Hungarian Jews out of economic and professional life.

Nazification of Czechoslokavia would hit only 36,000 Jews (.28 per cent of the population). The Jews are unevenly distributed there, the greater part living in the subcarpathian provinces. Up to now anti-Semitism is found only in the Sudeten German regions. Jews enjoy equal legal rights— Czechoslovakia still being a real democracy.

But the Jews living in the subcarpathian provinces are desperately poor—80 per cent of them literally on the verge of starvation; and, of course, one cannot know what the Nazis would do if they ever had a say in Czechoslovakia.

The only country in the Danube Basin where a Jewish persecution does not seem likely, in spite of propaganda, is Jugoslavia. There are 75,000 Jews there, but they form only 0.55 per cent of

the population, enjoy equal rights, play an important part in the economic development of the country and have never been considered a problem.

In the two Eastern European countries where
anti-Semitism is most acute, the race issue, if it
plays any role at all, is merely used as a pretext. In
Poland the reasons for discrimination against the
Jews are largely economic. In Rumania they are
largely political.

There are around 800,000 Jews in Rumania
(5 per cent of the population). Eighty per cent of
them earn their living in industry and commerce,
where they are very successful, and 2.5 per cent live
by agriculture. The passionate anti-Semitism, which
flared up in Rumania in the last years, is fostered
by the "Iron Guard," the Rumanian Nazi group,
who in large part are of peasant origin. They envy
the Jews' financial success. They resent Jewish in-
fluences in the King's inner circle. They hate especially the Transylvanian Jews, who, happy as they
were under three generations of Hapsburg tolerance, still feel themselves to be Hungarians, though
Transylvania has been transferred to Rumania.

In December, 1937, the Goga Government introduced anti-Semitic legislation and declared that
it would rid itself of the bulk of its Jewish population. At that, the late Mr. Goga, who was a poet and

incidentally had translated the Jewish poet Heine into Rumanian, was no Iron Guardist; on the contrary, by means of his anti-Semitic policy he hoped to steal the Iron Guards' thunder. Anyway, his policy became in a few weeks so unpopular with the Western democracies, and so menacing to Rumanian credit, that Mr. Goga had to resign.

When King Carol became his own dictator the anti-Semitic policy was at least temporarily suspended. The Iron Guard was disbanded. Still, King Carol does not make a secret of his conviction that there are too many Jews in Rumania and that the world should help him get rid of at least a few hundred thousand of them.

THE POLISH PROBLEM

Poland has a population of 35,000,000 in an essentially agricultural country, 3,500,000, or 10 per cent, being Jews. Poland suffers from a falling standard of living caused by a rapidly growing population and contracting outlets for labor and food markets.

Estimates have been made according to which one-third of the Polish population is surplus. Theoretically, surplus does not mean absolute over-population. It means only excess above what is required in relation to a given system of production. But can this system be changed in practice? In Poland any intensifying of farming would require irrigation schemes and therefore large capital investments. The same is true for large-scale industrialization. It is said that there are three possible adjustments to the present situation in Poland: one, mass industrialization; two, mass starvation; three, mass migration. And, experts believe that in order to realize the first and to avoid the second, the third is inevitable.

Of the 3,500,000 Polish Jews, one-tenth are engaged in agriculture. Only 40,000 earn their living in the professions and public services. The rest are traders and artisans.

It is estimated that only 700,000 of the Polish Jews make a fair living. One quarter (875,000) are semi-independent; another quarter could be rehabilitated with some external aid; and the remaining 30 per cent (1,050,000) are reduced to charity or to the necessity of emigrating.

Because there are so many of them and because the poor gentiles suspect that with fewer Jewish competitors they might be somewhat less poor, the Jewish problem has been acute since the establishment of the Polish State.

In the last two years—owing to the agitation of the National Democrats—anti-Jewish riots have increased. Many Jews have suffered violence—and many more live in constant fear of physical danger.

While the Polish Government officially maintains the equality of the Jews with all other Polish citizens, it sets about—in its quiet way—to squeeze the Jews out of economic life, mainly by means of tax and credit policies directed against commerce and trade, which especially hit the Jews. Only 15.9 per cent of the national income is derived from commerce, yet the tax paid by tradesmen amounts to 35.6 per cent of the total proceeds of the income tax. The state banks supply agriculture and the cooperatives with nearly ten times as much credit as they grant to commerce. Moreover, Poland is developing along the lines of state-owned and state-controlled industry, which already in 1931 made up 22.5 per cent of Poland's entire banking and industry, and has increased since. The number of Jews employed in government trading monopolies and plants is negligible, and each time a new business comes under government control, it means loss of jobs for Jews.

No wonder that the emigration movement has many followers among the Polish Jews! Half of the post-war Jewish immigration into Palestine was from Poland, and illegal immigration by Polish Jews into neighboring, and even into distant, countries is à l'ordre du jour.

I have said that according to estimate one-third

of the Polish population is surplus population. I have said, too, that back in the twenties, Dr. Nansen and Albert Thomas were convinced that countries such as Poland would have to get rid of some of their surplus population, somehow.

Quite understandably Jewish circles in America and elsewhere look at this question from a different point of view. Most of them feel that the sheer admission of the fact of the surplus population would present the Polish Government with too easy an excuse for getting rid of its Jews. And those who go so far as to admit the existence of the surplus don't like the notion that the government identifies this surplus with the Jewish minority.

This, they argue, establishes the Jews as second-rate citizens.

I am sure that humanitarians like Dr. Nansen and Albert Thomas never connected any such valuation with their conception of surplus population, and therefore implied no discrimination.

Obviously, if something is wrong about the surplus population it is economic circumstances, not the men, women and children who make the surplus up and who are probably no better and no worse than any other group. The facts, at any rate, must be contemplated. At least 1,200,000 Jews in Poland live in utter misery, and another 800,000 are hopelessly poor. These people would rather emigrate today than tomorrow, not because it would please the Polish Government, but because emigration is their only chance.

I am conscious of the fact that Jewish circles in the United States and elsewhere object for various reasons to planning Jewish emigration from Poland. One of their objections is that they thus would unwillingly justify the policy of forced Jewish emigration everywhere in the world.

This objection does not seem valid to me. Because they could not make a living in their own country hundreds of thousands of non-Jewish Polish workmen voluntarily went to France even in times when the economic situation was better than it is today. Because they could not make a living, hundreds of thousands of Polish Jews were charges of charity—especially of American-Jewish charity— even in the years directly following the establishment of the Polish Republic when the Jews enjoyed unrestricted political and economic equality.

There is no doubt in my mind that the young generation of Polish Jews would be much healthier standing on their own feet in a new country instead of staying in Poland and making each of their babies a potential candidate for charity from relatives or Jewish organizations abroad.

Another reason for objection among American and foreign Jewish circles to planning Jewish emigration from Poland lies in their apprehension that the mere existence of such plans might incite the Polish Government to put pressure on the Jews. I do not share this apprehension. On the contrary, I believe that the very fact that something is being done to enable emigration will materially change Polish policy toward the Jews. The Polish Government contends that it is unable to master its population problem all by itself. It contends that it depends on outside cooperation. And such outside cooperation, if offered to it, will induce it to abolish or at least to soften some of the measures which at present are especially oppressive.

Obviously, the fact that the Polish Republic is unable to create enough work for its people does not justify its Government in pressing Jewish emigration. The Polish Government can, however, expect a certain understanding of the existing problem and a cooperation toward a solution which it is unable to work out alone.

ATTEMPTS AT JEWISH MASS SETTLEMENT

There have been made, up to the present, three practical experiments in Jewish mass settlement.

One is the Agrojoint settlement in the Ukraine, which was started in the twenties, and financed by funds of the Joint Distribution Committee. It was, in fact, the only political venture of this otherwise altogether philanthrophic organization. According to the figures given by the IDC, 250,000 Jews have been settled there on 3,000,000 acres of land. Unfortunately reality presents itself less sanguinely than these figures. It is not so much that bad harvests ruined the Agrojoint settlements economically; there was always new money available to be pumped into them. It was rather that almost from the start these settlements had an unfortunate effect on the relationship between the Ukrainian Government and population, on the one hand, and the Jewish settlers on the other hand.

Less and less the latter fitted into the economic structure of Soviet Russia, which tried to eliminate the Kulak and to destroy racial and religious group life. The famine of 1932 and the growing agricultural collectivization drove away a great percentage of the settlers—40 per cent has been estimated—but these figures cannot be substantiated. Many were deported and some were killed. As things stand, the Agrojoint settlements are without importance in a consideration of future Jewish mass settlement.

Things are different in Birobidjan. Birobidjan,

the Soviet Government declared, should be a real
Jewish state within the USSR, a socialist Jewish
homeland for Jews all over the world who were
for socialism and for a homeland. But somehow
nothing much came of this plan. Up to now, only
12,000 Jews are settled in Birobidjan—and at the
present time Russia has stopped Jewish immigration there altogether. The Soviet Government was
probably afraid of getting in elements who would
prove politically troublesome in a region which, in
view of its closeness to the Manchurian border, is
strategically important. But even if the Russian
authorities should lift the immigration ban, the unfortunate location of Birobidjan—open to any at-
tack from the Japanese—does not augur much good
for the Jewish State in the USSR.

The third practical experiment is Palestine. In
the first years after the promulgation of Hitler's
anti-Semitic policies in Germany, most of the efforts
of world Jewry to direct the flood of Jewish emigration from Germany centered on Palestine. Even
the Jews who had been sceptical about the success
of the "Jewish homeland" and who had been afraid
that the existence of a Jewish National State might
be made a pretext for casting suspicion upon the
loyalty of Jews everywhere toward the nations in
which they were citizens—even these Jews were

happy that here the persecuted could find a refuge.

Between 1933 and the beginning of 1938, 42,000 German Jews emigrated to Palestine, which brought the total of the Jewish population there to about 400,000 as against an Arab population of 942,000. But a coincident growth of Arab hostility, culminating in a guerrilla war, made it evident that the abrupt rise of Jewish immigration since 1933 had produced a crisis in which the whole question of the Jewish homeland would have to be reconsidered.

In the summer of 1937 a British Royal Commission decided that the Arab claim of self-government and the secure establishment of a Jewish National Home in Palestine were incompatible. It reported that the mandate was unworkable, and that the only solution was the partition of Palestine, by which the Jews would be left merely a tiny country of their own. The pros and cons of this plan are still being hotly discussed in Jewish and Arabian circles. It appears today that the more politically minded among the Zionists believe that the partition—though by no means an ideal solution—is the best that can be hoped for under the circumstances.

The Arabs, on the contrary, show growing opposition against having even a small Jewish state in their midst.

No decision has been made yet. The British Government first announced that as long as the fate of the mandate is in the balance, Jewish immigration would be allowed to continue at a rate not exceeding the annual figure of 12,000 suggested by the Royal Commission.

This policy, it appears, is being modified, as the immigration schedule for the six months from April 1st, 1938, to September 30th, 1938, provides that the "maximum aggregate number of foreigners" who will be permitted to enter the country as immigrants is 3,670. Eleven hundred and fifty of these 3,670 will hold labor certificates, 180 of which however are destined for laborers who entered temporarily two years ago and the period of whose residence has now expired. Certificates for "capitalists" included in the aggregate figure amount to 2,020. Students and relatives are excluded from the quota restrictions. The certificates permit the immigrants to bring their families.

Whatever the final outcome of the Palestine crisis—whether the partition scheme goes through and a diminutive Jewish State is founded, or whether Jews are allowed to settle in an undivided Palestine until they constitute a minority of 35 per cent, or even 40 per cent of the total population—one thing seems certain: all hopes of anything like Jewish mass emigration to Palestine have to be buried.

While the Arabs may not succeed in stopping Jewish immigration altogether, we must assume that it will not exceed the present limited quota, which, of course, is utterly inadequate to solve the problem of the Jews of Germany and Eastern Europe in the present emergency. We must face the fact that the fiery nationalism of the Arabs is growing more and more aggressive.

This is deeply regrettable. The Jewish settlement work done in Palestine is admirable, the racial and moral effect it has had on the settling Jews alone being something to behold, especially as far as the Jews in the agricultural communities are concerned. There, the sons and daughters of the persecuted Eastern Jews grow up to be healthy creatures who do not bear the stigma of their Jewishness any more, but feel themselves to be free and happy human beings. There is no doubt that many of the Jews in Palestine and of those who want to emigrate to Palestine are prepared to take the risk of insecurity and to fight and die for a country which they consider their homeland.

Still, unless the difficulties between Arabs and

Jews can be cleared up and a reconciliation effected, Palestine must be considered as a danger spot for the Jews from which—at least for the moment—no solution can be expected for the problem of Jewish refugees.

CHAPTER FOUR

This Still Empty World

WHENEVER the problem of actual or potential refugees is discussed, somebody will ask: "Yes—but where can they go?" More often than not this question is meant to close the discussion, the "but" indicating that, sympathetic as we may be toward the refugees, we are helpless, as the world is practically full, or at least closed.

The conception is erroneous. The world is by no means over-populated. And if it is closed, it only shows the ineffectiveness of the economic and political systems under which we live, and the unreasonableness, the lack of imagination and daring, by which we sin against more than one great problem of our times.

There are many countries and colonial regions, which, if they are to make the most of their potentialities, will need to augment their populations for decades to come. Furthermore, the white population of the Western world is, as a whole, declining, and the fact is a cause of concern to our vital statisticians and our eugenists. This is true of the United States where except in a few areas, notably the deep South, the population is rapidly approaching the point where it will become stable, and thereafter decline.

And there are many experts, and by no means the least persuasive, who trace part of the economic ills of this country, including unemployment and economic instability recorded in depression periods following each other in quick succession, not to the fact that we have too many people but to the fact that we have not an expanding population which would continually increase the demand for basic necessities.

These too few people, to be sure, are accumulated in and around great cities. Vast regions lie, for sheer emptiness, cut off and atrophied. According to these experts what this country needs is a decentralization of production, and more and better trained man power to create and consume wealth.

IMMIGRANTS: ASSETS OR LIABILITIES?

The theory that new immigrants necessarily detract from the economic life of a country, instead of adding to it, has validity only if the new immigration is allowed to accumulate in a few congested areas, to become stranded there, and so to add to already existing unemployment.

Actually, thousands of those who now are potential immigrants have added immensely to the economic prosperity of the countries which they wish to leave, and under advantageous circumstances—under a carefully selected, planned, and financed immigration system—could bring to a new country resources of skill which would increase its wealth and its trade.

At this moment, for instance, whole Austrian industries are seeking new foundations in other countries because the organizers and the workers of these industries can no longer operate in their own land, for reasons which are not economic but political.

Vienna's fame for industries and crafts based on artistic taste and careful and highly trained skills has been rivaled only by that of Paris. Every year millions of dollars have been paid by this country for imports of Viennese goods, either directly or through the purchases of tourists. Furthermore these goods have an already existing international clientele. It would be relatively easy to make America the center of these particular industries today, thereby keeping at home millions now spent abroad, and, at the same time, opening lines for a profitable new export trade, particularly in South America.

Viennese industrialists might not only bring over their trained employees, who would compete with no class of workers in existence in America, but also their lists of customers, and their knowledge of foreign markets, which, up to now, have never been within American reach. This sort of industry, which does not compete with any existing American industry, which does not depend upon large and expensive machinery, and products of which are easily transportable, is admirably adapted to small centers.

Consider, for example, the paraphernalia and clothes associated with the sport of skiing, in which Austrian technicians and outfitters have long led the way.

WHERE IMMIGRANTS COULD GO

It is significant that lately there has been a new interest in immigration in Canada, where since 1930 immigration of all except relatives of already established settlers has been stopped. Now demands have been made that the bars should be let down, and an aggressive policy of immigration launched. This has been especially favored by the railway companies who hope that Canada's per capita debt and railway deficit can be reduced if there are more heads by which to divide them. They estimate that new freight traffic created by successful settlers is worth about four hundred dollars per head per year.

Canadian circles interested in immigration emphasize that a settlement must be carefully planned and directed, the question being not one of finding sufficient land capable of sustaining individual farm families, but chiefly of meeting initial community costs for education, transportation, and civil government. According to Mr. W. A. Mackintosh,* immigration to Canada could advantageously reach an average of 100,000 people per year.

Mr. Griffith Taylor * admits that the "vast potentialities" of the "Empty Spaces" in Australia exist only in the minds of ignorant boosters, but he contends that the southeast quarter of the continent where at present only 6,000,000 are settled is one of the best areas for white settlement in the world and could support 20,000,000 were Australia developed to the same extent as the United States, and that the full development of natural resources would require an even greater increase.

* See Limits of Land Settlement—Isaiah Bowman (Council on Foreign Relations—New York).

As for Africa, the estimates of the potential "carrying capacity" vary between one and two billions. A. Fischer predicts the greatest possible increase for inner Africa (between the Sahara and the Zambezi), where the natural conditions are thought to be capable of supporting a population of one and a half billions instead of the present total of seventy-nine millions. These figures sound fantastic, considering the unreliability of rainfall, the spread of malaria and other tropical diseases, and the problem of native labor, all of which make life difficult for present settlers. The experts, of course, base their gigantic figures on the expectation that the matter of rainfall can be taken care of by scientific methods; that tropical diseases will disappear with the introduction of sanitary measures; and that the question of labor will be solved by sheer reasonableness. They contend that all this has its best chance with the development of European settlements.

THE POSSIBILITIES IN BRAZIL

The country which offers the greatest possibilities for mass settlement is Brazil. According to conservative estimates, Brazil, excluding the Amazon forest, is able to contain and support 395,000,000 people. Its present population is 44,000,000. Notwithstanding the existing immigration bars, every Brazilian statesman, diplomat and businessman will confide to you that what his country needs is a few million more inhabitants.

The following is from a report of a recent field study on the possibility of settlement in Brazil:

"Brazil is in this exceptional situation: alone among the great immigration countries, it has still, after fifty years of large-scale immigration, an enormous area of undeveloped land of great fertility, situated in zones in which the European can easily become acclimatized. It is this abundance of land which has permitted Brazil to receive and keep many millions of immigrants in the past, and which justifies the expectation that, despite the present check on migration movements caused by the depression and other circumstances, the overpopulated countries will continue to make large and valuable contributions to the population in the future. But while it is true that millions of men could find in Brazil today a plot of land sufficient to feed them and a house to shelter them (timber for building is available close at hand in almost every part of the country), emigrants prepared to ask no more than the satisfaction of these elementary needs are almost impossible to find in the emigration countries of Europe. Further, their establishment in Brazil in such primitive conditions would contribute nothing to the economic prosperity of the country—on the contrary, it would act as a dead weight hampering the social progress which every organized community must promote. In other words, in order that settlement may not be foredoomed to failure, there must be a chance, however small, of selling part of the produce of the land, and so, by exchange, of obtaining the goods and services essential to a civilized life." *

REQUIREMENTS FOR RESETTLEMENT

But if colonization is to be successful, expert planning in advance is required, and a considerable outlay of capital. All the settlements which failed during the last twenty years—I pointed this out in connection with the half-hearted experiments of the League of Nations—failed for lack of planning, or for lack of funds or for lack of both.

Plans must take into account not only the degree to which land in a given country is vacant, but also whether modern tools and methods are available, what are the market and transport facilities, the climatic conditions, etc.—and especially the immigrants' economic and social adaptability.

Of all the elements which enter into the problem of settlement, that which needs most planning is

* Isaiah Bowman, in "Limits of Land Settlement."

the settler himself. He must not only have the physical fitness and the economic training necessary for his new environment, he must have confidence in his own strength and he must have patience. He must be prepared to work hard and to sacrifice at least part of the present for some future benefit. In a word: he must have the pioneer spirit.

It is said that the pioneer spirit has disappeared from the world and that people are too spoiled to endure the hard life of the frontier. I do not believe this is true. The pioneer spirit has not disappeared in the twentieth century. It has only changed from what it was in the nineteenth and eighteenth centuries. In these earlier periods, when the whole world was primarily agricultural, the settler could go to any country where there was vacant land, often in a climate not too much unlike that of his homeland, without giving up much in the way of physical comforts. He had not been used at home to having a telephone, easily available medical care, and easily available amusements in the form of radio or the movies.

Today the gap between the homeland—any homeland—and the frontier, as far as technical things go, is much greater.

Almost all potential immigration countries are on a lower technological level than the one which the settler has been used to. Naturally, the immigrant has the desire to attain as quickly as possible the degree of civilization he has been accustomed to at home.

But it does not follow from this that the immigrant is too soft, or that he is unfit for pioneering work. On the contrary, as might be concluded from the above-quoted report about settlement in Brazil, the settler's demand for the advantages of civilization will actually prove to be his greatest asset to the country where he settles.

If any one example could confound the defeatist attitude, it is the work of the Eastern Jews in Palestine. Crushed and humiliated for generations, they seemed the worst possible material for pioneering; but in a very few years they have demonstrated their capacity to re-train themselves—more, even to change their physical type.

THE NEW FRONTIER

Nor is the frontier of the twentieth century what it was in the eighteenth and nineteenth centuries. The frontier has changed as much as the pioneer. Most of the frontier areas today, in order to be able to compete with the rest of the world, depend on large scale technological advance rather than on old-fashioned individual pioneering.

The refugees and those who concern themselves with their fate cannot afford to indulge in sentimentality. They must realize that no country is willing to receive settlers for charity's sake, but that it will expect its new settlers to bring it irrigation, electrification, swamp-clearing, roads, railways, schools, the most modern systems of hygiene, etc. It will expect new settlers to develop their new homeland not only with all their own individual pioneering spirit, but also with all the old country's attainments in. technical and scientific lines.

That is why mass settlement in our times will work out only if it takes the form of community settlement. Immigrants must have housing, gas, water, electricity, hospitals and schools. Only in technically highly developed communities can the twentieth century pioneers do their best. And only communities of this kind can reward adequately the lands which have received them and given them homes.

Obviously, the essential condition to any solution of the refugee problem is to divest it of the stigma of charity. In times like ours, native populations are afraid of newcomers; if the presence of the latter does not prove a definite asset, the consequences will be disastrous in the extreme. Those who concern themselves with the fate of refugees will not be able to rest on their laurels once they succeed in getting them out of the country where they are oppressed, and into some new country. It is at that point that the real task starts for the refugees as well as for their helpers—the task of making the immigration project productive and constructive for everybody. This takes, I repeat, collective effort. Above all, I repeat, it needs large funds.

For settling people successfully in new homes, one needs money, money and again money.

CHAPTER FIVE

Towards a Practical Program *

THE ROOSEVELT ACTION

IN MARCH, 1938, President Roosevelt, moved no doubt by the sudden creation of a new refugee problem through the German conquest of Austria, sent out an appeal to the countries of the world to join with the United States in trying to formulate a new practical international policy to deal with the problem of refugees. The impulse was generous and practical. Thirty-two countries including all the great and small democracies of Europe, the South American republics and the four Dominions of the British Commonwealth responded affirmatively and agreed to send delegates to a conference which will prob-

* The plan outlined in this chapter developed largely through conversations with Moritz Schlesinger, a close friend of the late Fridtjof Nansen, with whom he collaborated in the repatriation of the prisoners of the World War. Later he was appointed representative of the League of Nations for refugees, joining Dr. Nansen in his relief work. Mr. Schlesinger, as a former German Consul General and an adviser to the German Government on Eastern affairs up to 1933 was responsible for the credit system on which German Soviet trade relations have been based.

ably be held before this book is published, in Evian in France.

The American delegate to this conference is Mr. Myron C. Taylor, who for this purpose enjoys the rank of Ambassador. Mr. Taylor is a man of international background, and great organizing capacity, who was until recently President of the United States Steel Corporation. He will be assisted by two experts from our own State Department. At the same time President Roosevelt has appointed an American Committee headed by Mr. James G. McDonald, and including representatives of many American organizations already interested in the problem.

The President's appeal, this conference, and the organization which it is hoped will result from it are the most hopeful signs in years that some form of constructive international action may be undertaken. The appeal and the conference have raised hope again in the breasts of many in whom it had died. Thousands look to this conference as the arbiter of their destinies. Thousands pray fervently to God that out of this move will emerge a more courageous, competent, coordinated, inclusive, and practical plan for dealing with a leading world issue.

It would be a real catastrophe, both for the *emigrés* and for the democratic nations if the President's action should result only in propaganda, raise false hopes, and end up by being only a Kellogg Pact for refugees, and about as effective as the Kellog Pact has proved itself to be.

Firm resolutions passed by the governments of the democratic powers would undoubtedly be useful. But a large scale international program, worked out to the last practical detail, is essential. What needs to be done is to obtain the consent of particular governments to make particular financial arrangements and the consent of other governments to take immigrants. We need the establishment of an authoritative and continuous office with representatives in the various capitals of emigration and immigration countries and we need the establishment of a finance corporation.

There is at present no other organization in the world which offers this hope. It may be presumed that the Nansen Committee now merged with the High Commission for Refugees coming from Germany will continue to concern itself with the legal and political destinies of exiles. But this will probably be the limit of its action. It will give no advice or help to prospective refugees—those who are still in the countries of their nativity but who are forced to contemplate emigration within the immediate future. Nor can we expect the Nansen Committee to help these people to find a place to go nor to arrange ways through which they will find work, nor to establish means by which they will become financial assets to their new homes, nor to stabilize existences which are utterly precarious.

Without doubt the Roosevelt conference will establish cooperation with the Nansen Office, starting action where the competence of the Nansen Office leaves off.

CATEGORIES OF REFUGEES

Any plan set up by the conference must distinguish between two categories of refugees: those who, owing to connections abroad or the ownership of transferable property, are able to choose their new country and to emigrate individually; and those—by far the greater number—who have no means or connections abroad, cannot choose their new country and have to leave either their native country or whatever place in which they may have found a temporary domicile.

The first group comprises a great many refugees who are eminent intellectuals, especially skilled. Their problem is to find work that will not dislodge native intellectual workers or natives working in the professions or trades. Insofar as the refugees belong to the free professions this is a matter of competition, with everything at the outset to the natives' advantage—particularly language.

It is a mistake to believe that every new brain worker dislodges someone else. Many of the refugees from Vienna, for instance, are unique, possessed of skills or special knowledge which every country, the United States included, can use. There are, for instance, branches of medical research that have been better explored in Vienna than anywhere else in the world. Their explorers are now exiles and will be an asset to any country that receives them.

The Viennese intellectuals, especially the younger ones, are unique in that many of them have been trained in manual work and are willing to do it. I know an eminent architect who also happens to be a highly skilled bricklayer—and is willing to lay bricks in a new home. Also there are hundreds of skilled artisans seeking immigration visas, who, if organized, could transplant to other soils various industries which represent right now millions of dollars' worth of annual trade.

As far as our own country is concerned, it is necessary to distribute these individuals as widely as possible throughout the continent. Nothing will be in the long run more dangerous for the refugees themselves than to increase the white collar proletariat, and evoke fear among those whose struggle for survival is already desperate, thus transplanting the resentments from which they are in flight.

This is an organizational task of great scope and importance. The philanthropic organizations which try to fulfill it now dispose neither of sufficient means nor of a personnel schooled for the purpose of adapting the abilities of the immigrants to the needs of the new country. This task must be put into the hands of leading personalities in science and industry, who will seek out really competent sub-personnel. It cannot be done by amateurs.

As for the second category—they are a problem for mass settlement and that can only be successful if it is exceedingly well prepared and well financed. This involves a tremendous organizational effort, and will, we hope, represent the main task of the Roosevelt action.

WHAT A SOLUTION DEMANDS

Immediate plans, therefore, whether undertaken as a whole by the Roosevelt action or coordinated through it, ought to include the setting up of a Re-settlement Cooperation on a business basis. That is the first thing that has to be done. Its practical activities would be numerous, and the organization involved grandiose.

They would include, presumably, numerous services in connection both with emigration and immigration countries. These services would require a personnel of two sorts: personalities of such prestige and with such support from their own governments that they would command attention in important negotiations; and technical experts familiar with the complexities and details of the problems involved.

For instance, a service is required to advise prospective emigrants. Such a service, I think, ought to be established in the capitals of emigration countries. Its business would be to advise prospective emigrants of the possibilities abroad and of the physical, political, and training demands that other countries are making. This service would also supervise the selection of emigrants for specific destinations and specific community settlements. It would serve both those emigrants who wish and are able to adjust themselves individually to their new country and those who are leaving *en masse*.

Organization is also needed in the immigration countries, to submit proposals to the international organization regarding the possibility of mass settlement in their respective countries, and the conditions which the immigrants would have to fulfill.

A service is also needed for refugees in the capitals of countries where the refugees have unequal rights as compared with the native population. This service, which might be carried out by the Nansen Office or in collaboration with it, would be concerned with obtaining passports, re-entry permits, permits of domicile, and labor permits. It would be essentially a legal service.

And a service is needed for individual refugees in the countries of immigration.

This service ought first of all to consider means of alleviating the difficulties under the existing immigration laws of every country, and to formulate ways for making the mechanism more elastic. Under present conditions in the United States, refugees on visitor's visas—and this includes many of the more competent individuals who are perfectly able to take care of themselves—must leave the country and re-enter on the quota if they wish to stay. The whole process is tremendously cumbersome and expensive for the immigrant and serves only a formal purpose, for no one leaves to re-enter on an immigration visa until he has fully ascertained that he will be granted a number and allowed to do so. But the process of leaving and re-entering, under present conditions, involves a trip to Cuba or to Mexico and the expenditure of hundreds of dollars where a whole family is concerned. It might be considered whether immigration visas for those already here on visitor's visas might not be granted in Washington, instead of distant consulates, with a little more care exercised in granting the original visitor's visas and with arrangements to record the port of entry in them.

This would save much to those refugees who prefer to explore personally the possibilities of a country on their own responsibility before they decide where to settle down.

Also, individual immigration can be alleviated in the United States—and all this without any revision of the present quota laws—by allowing the affidavits of relatives to be replaced by the affidavits of friends or responsible organizations willing to put up bonds or other securities.

This particular service is also needed to coordinate the work of existing agencies, to work in close cooperation with intellectual and industrial associations and labor unions.

This service inside the countries of immigration ought also to concern itself with the distribution of refugees, exploring the possibilities in all the provincial centers; finding out what new industries could be established with European skills that would not compete with existing industries, and thus working to prevent the accumulation of new immigrants in already overcrowded centers where the competition for jobs is most virulent, remembering that an undirected immigration may augment hostility against aliens. These services in the various countries should be in connection with each other for the purpose of mutual information about possibilities of immigration and work. What needs to be avoided is the splitting up of the various forces dealing with this problem.

There is also needed a service for the re-training of *emigrés* to equip themselves for new lives, and often new pursuits, under new circumstances. The example of Palestine has demonstrated that this is possible—that it is possible for men and women who have hitherto been engaged in commercial or intellectual pursuits to re-train themselves for agriculture and for different forms of social existence.

THE GREAT TASK—FINANCING

But the great task of the Roosevelt conference, or whatever organization it sets up, is to find means of financing this whole endeavor.

The funds needed for transporting and settling hundreds of thousands of people successfully are gigantic. Therefore, any plan that hopes to solve the refugee problem must first of all examine how these funds are to be raised.

CHARITY IS NOT ENOUGH

Obviously, they cannot be raised by charity drives or voluntary donations by individuals and organizations alone. Not even the most generous Jewish charity, which time and again has so magnificently risen to the occasion, and which puts Christian charity to shame, has been able or will be able to meet the total financial demands of refugees of Jewish faith—to say nothing of the demands of refugees who are not Jewish. This is not news. It was pointed out by Mr. James McDonald when he resigned in 1935 as High Commissioner for Refugees coming from Germany. And it is even truer now than it was then.

Charity is not and cannot be enough. Nor is it likely that one can count on private finance alone, although a more enterprising spirit in private capitalism would discover now, as in the days of the East India Company, vast possibilities for profit in the settlement in pioneer countries of men and women and youths of superior training and diversified talents. The capitalist world keeps billions of money lying idle in safes rather than chance new investments. Its imagination is dulled. It no longer sees visions. Can that be one reason for its failing profits? An enlightened twentieth century imperialism would realize that all wealth derives from

labor applied to natural resources and would itself
devise financial inventions to bring together unex-
ploited territories, highly cultivated European skills,
and the passionate need for new homes. Today, as
in the past, these might be the foundations for
whole new civilizations.

It ought to be possible to form an international
corporation which could raise in the open market,
on a strictly commercial basis, adequate capital for a
really grandiose international scheme for developing backward territories with displaced Europeans,
recognizing that there is available, at this moment,
for resettlement purposes, a kind and character of
labor which has not been emigrating for generations,
and which has the intellectual and moral equipment
to re-train itself—under, of course, direction.

MOBILIZE BLOCKED ACCOUNTS

But in a world dominated by theories of state
capitalism, this is hardly likely to happen, unless,
or until, the present trend is reversed. Meanwhile
there is another solution. It does not involve raising
a cent of new capital. All the money that is needed is
right at hand in the form of billions of dollars' worth
of blocked German marks, blocked Hungarian pen-
goes, blocked Rumanian leis, blocked Bulgarian
levas—and heaven knows how many other blocked

valutas. The funds belonging to emigrants and frozen in their native countries, or belonging to foreigners and frozen in countries where they have made investments, could be released for constructive resettlement purposes, and for the benefit of everybody concerned.

Consider only the blocked marks in Germany, belonging to foreign citizens. Nobody knows exactly how many there are, but it is safe to say that they amount to several billions of dollars. In good faith, for the benefit of themselves and of Germany, these foreigners invested their capital in Germany.

Today, with few exceptions, the foreign owners of blocked accounts cannot collect either the principal or interest of their investment. The only way in which they can realize on their property is to liquidate it in the open international market. The exchange now stands at about 5 cents for the blocked mark, so that a foreign owner who sells a blocked account of a million marks realizes only fifty thousand dollars.

The same, of course, is true of blocked funds belonging to emigrants. If they transfer their funds abroad at the present rate, they lose so much that only the immensely wealthy can salvage enough to help them build up a new existence.

Now, an international organization dealing with

the refugee probem, ought first of all to ascertain the possible means by which this blocked money can be put to work.

It must not be assumed that the German and other governments which have blocked the transfer of moneys cannot be brought into any sort of co-operation. On the contrary, it must be assumed that particularly those governments whose policies have created refugee problems can be persuaded that it is to their own interest to help solve these problems.

It is true that these governments have created so much bitterness that there are many people who are unwilling even to consider negotiating with them; that others are willing to negotiate but are convinced in advance that negotiations will be futile, that the governments in question are primarily interested in upsetting the world's stability and will maliciously sabotage any attempt to deal with the situations that have been created. Others argue that any plan for using blocked marks or any currency which increases exports from Germany or other countries is an aid to those countries, and helps the present regimes in those countries to survive.

It therefore becomes for the individual a question of whether one hates Nazi ideals more than one loves democratic principles; whether one still has faith in a theory of international economics such as Secretary Hull's, or whether one thinks the Fascist countries can be starved out—at the expense of the refugees.

I, for one, believe that the whole barter system which the controlled states have built up is so medieval and barbaric, so out of harmony with the realities of the modern world, that any program which can in any way make a dent in the closed systems and let in a little air, is devoutly to be welcomed. For either air will be let in, or eventually we shall all, refugees and non-refugees, Fascists and democrats alike, die slowly of economic attrition.

THE APPEAL TO REASON

I think that one can assume that in all the controlled economies there are people who know this, and people prepared to listen to reason, at least in a limited way. There is nothing fantastic about such an assumption. It is proved by the fact that cooperation is actually being successfully put into practice in the case of the settlement of German Jews in Palestine. I have already explained how this is being done. By means of a trade-and-transfer arrangement between the Nazi government and the Haavara, 82 million marks' worth of capital values have been transferred to Palestine in the last five years. All of this was transferred in the form of German export goods, the equivalent of which was credited to the immigrants in Palestine pounds. In this case, the cooperation consisted in the Nazi Government consenting to being paid for its export goods in blocked marks instead of in much-coveted foreign exchange, and in the Palestine importers giving up any idea of boycotting German goods.

It may be left to those who are only theoretically interested in the refugee problem to figure out what was uppermost in the Nazi Government's mind when it gave its consent to this arrangement—whether their interest was primarily in increasing their exports, or primarily in getting rid of their Jews. From a practical point of view the result only is important. The result has been that 14,000 refugee families have been enabled to settle in Palestine, taking along their own savings in the form of goods. The point to keep in mind is that they have been able to transfer their wealth, not in the form of consumer's goods, which would have no point, but in the form of capital goods—the means of production, the means of creating new wealth in another country and building a new modern civilization.

Quite understandably, Jewish circles in the

United States and elsewhere may not be wholly enthusiastic about any plan that aids the refugees by increasing exports from anti-Semitic countries. However, objections along this line imply a theory of economics which I cannot share. Is it better for German wealth to be used to help build up the technical civilization of the world, or to be frozen dead in German banks or used for German armaments? The pros and cons of the boycott as a political weapon need not be discussed here. But as an economic weapon, it is a denial of liberal principles. And on humanitarian grounds it is impossible to find an intellectually valid justification for it, unless the rest of the world is prepared to go the whole way and make a complete quarantine of the countries that are creating the problems.

And that involves the realization that that quarantine would operate, in the first line, against the persecuted.

If the democratic world were realistic and robust, it would regard the refugees as potential assets, provided the task of transfer and resettlement can be organized in a large way and with imagination and adequate finance. This in no way implies that one approves the policy which has made refugees of hundreds of thousands of innocent persons. It only implies that the free world is still adequate to meet even this artificially created problem.

TRANSFERRING CAPITAL GOODS

With the example of Palestine in mind, one can proceed on the assumption that, if the emigration countries are unwilling or unable to raise the *valuta* for the transfer of blocked funds in money, they are willing to transfer at least a fraction of these blocked funds in the form of industrial products and capital goods. And capital goods are better than nothing in any case, and are everything in un-developed countries whose technological future lies ahead of them. They are exactly what are needed for mass settlements in countries such as those of South America. And new mass settlements, on a decent standard of civilization, will create new markets for the whole world!

An example might clarify things. Let us say that a country X declares its willingness to take 50,000 refugees, whose settlement should take the form of founding one or several communities. If each of these 50,000 people commanded adequate savings they could emigrate individually, each on his own responsibility. But this, of course, is not the case. However, some of them will have funds sufficient to pay their own passage. For the rest, organizations must come to the rescue.

Fifty thousand is easily said and easily read. Fifty thousand refugees fill twenty-five big steamers to the last berth. Immense means are needed not only for the personal equipment of the individual refugee—his household goods, tools, etc.—but for all that the refugees need in order to build up a community that will make them welcome to the frontier of the twentieth century. In other words, they should have—according to the specific needs of the country and the region—gas, water, electric works, communal buildings, schools and the five to ten thousand houses which will serve as living quarters for fifty thousand people.

Let us assume that for the settlement of fifty thousand refugees $30,000,000 is needed. Of this, $20,000,000 might be brought into the country in the form of raw materials and industrial products and $10,000,000 might be given as a cash loan from the immigration country.

AN INTERNATIONAL RESETTLEMENT COMPANY

Let us talk first of how to get the $20,000,000!

Along strictly commercial lines a company could be formed which we will call here the "International Resettlement Company." Foreign citizens or emigrants with blocked funds—as an example, we will take Germany—would put at the disposal of this company a hundred millions in blocked marks at a discount of 50 per cent. Instead of these one hundred million Reichsmarks (valued, at the *official* foreign exchange rate, at $40,000,000) the owners of the blocked accounts would receive from the company $20,000,000 in bonds. Considering all facts, this is an excellent compromise for the owner of blocked accounts. For, as I have already pointed out, at the present *actual* exchange rate of 5 cents for the blocked mark, the outright sale of a hundred million marks would only bring $5,000,000.

This amount of $5,000,000, however, would actually be assured in five years as interest on a $20,-000,0000 loan to the "International Resettlement Company" at a rate of 5 per cent.

This interest would be paid in the amount of $1,000,000 yearly, which is the equivalent of 5 per cent interest on the $20,000,000 worth of bonds. Therefore, at the end of five years, the owners of the originally blocked marks would receive not only $5,000,000, which is the value of the blocked marks on the open market today, but would also have $20,000,000 worth of bonds, their value represented by the wealth of the growing community they have helped to found.

Inasmuch as blocked marks are constantly being devalued today, their investment in this manner is definitely advantageous.

However, the exchange of a hundred million blocked marks into a loan to the "International Re-settlement Company" is only then attractive to the owners, if the 5 per cent interest for five years is really secured.

HOW TO GUARANTEE INTEREST

Now, there are several possible ways of securing this interest. For instance, the charity organizations which are now spending yearly millions of dollars for inadequate returns, might secure part of it, and in this way mobilize much greater funds that they could otherwise secure.

THE POSSIBLE MOBILIZATION OF WAR DEBTS

And is it chimerical to suggest that while we are dealing with one category of unproductive debts we might also take advantage of another unproductive debt situation to help our work forward and thus turn an obstacle to political understanding into a factor of international pacification?

The British Government, for example, owes the American Government a great deal of money—to be exact, $4,600,000,000, plus unpaid interest of $818,000,000 computed from the date of funding in 1923 to November, 1937.

Suppose it were proposed to the British that, as they are unwilling to receive any considerable number of refugees, and as they would doubtless like to contribute somehow toward a solution of the refugee problem, they put up a certain sum of money as security for the interest on the settlement loans— we to credit that sum as a payment on the war debt. The sum of $5,000,000, for example, would cover interest payments for five years on a loan of $20,-000,000 at five per cent. And a loan of that magnitude would enable fifty thousand refugees to undertake a new existence in a new land. The sacrifice involved for the United States in remitting $5,000,000 on a debt of nearly five and a half billions would not be, to put it mildly, severe. And the British would not pay a penny which they do not owe anyway.

Under an arrangement between Germany and the "International Resettlement Company" similar to the one between Germany and the Haavara on behalf of the Palestine settlement, all the goods needed for settling a community of fifty thousand refugees in a given country would be paid for with a hundred million blocked marks. As actually this hundred million marks cost only fifty millions, the price of the German goods would not exceed world market prices. The value of the goods bought in Germany would correspond to the dollar value of the bonds, and the financial structure of the enterprise would be on a sound commercial basis right from the start.

The sum of $20,000,000 would equip the fifty thousand refugees in a manner to make them welcome settlers in any frontier land.

In order to tide them over for the first period of their stay in the new countries, to enable them to get constructive work going, they would need a cash advance on their wages. It might take the form of a loan by the immigration country. The security for this loan could be the goods imported by the refugees. The enhanced value of the cultivated soil, the creation of water and electric power, would make the loan increasingly profitable to the immigration country.

How much healthier it would be, if engineers, technicians, artisans, farmers, teachers, doctors should emigrate, sure of finding their place in a new community than if they arrive individually, received at the pier by relatives who, while rejoicing over the rescue of one dear to them, are already worrying about how to find him a job!

I cannot discuss here the details of the arrangements that would have to be made between emigration countries and immigration countries. I have merely set out to demonstrate that it is possible by cooperation to raise the gigantic funds needed for mastering the refugee problem. The sources exist in the form of blocked accounts of natives and foreigners in emigration countries, and, perhaps also in the debts which the United States has outstanding in Great Britain and elsewhere all over the world.

Many combinations of the example given for financing the settlement of fifty thousand German refugees in the country X are possible. So, for instance, if the needed goods consist of wood or oil and cannot be bought in Germany, the "International Resettlement Company" can use the blocked accounts of foreign citizens in Poland for buying the wood, and the blocked accounts of foreign citizens in Rumania for buying oil.

The same arrangement that in our example allowed England to deduct the amount of £1,-000,000 from its war debt, if it puts up this amount for securing the interest on the resettlement loan, can be made for any country that is indebted to the United States—and aren't most of them?

Suppose the American Congress would be willing to recognize $25,000,000 put up for the purpose of securing the interest on the refugee loans by the debtor countries, as repayment on the war debts. Suppose the various debtor countries divide these $25,000,000 among themselves. The burden for the budget of the individual country would be negligible, poor as the country may be. The "International Resettlement Company," on the other hand, would be enabled to buy 500,000,000 blocked marks or corresponding sums in other *valuta*, and to emigrate and settle 250,000 refugees. These refugees would not come as undesirable destitute fugitives, dependent on the charity of private organizations, but as welcome settlers equipped with everything to enrich the new country and to help in developing a new civilization.

We can afford to consider this financial scheme, intricate as it may seem to the layman, with a certain degree of confidence. There is certainly the possibility that on a sound commercial basis blocked funds can be had for settlement purpose. There is no doubt that governments which control relatively empty territories, and which now do not welcome miscellaneous immigrants, would change their minds if these immigrants were carefully selected and equipped in advance to become self-supporting and productive citizens.

As for the governments which are now forcing emigration, one must hope that they will in their hearts welcome a plan of cooperation.

Even the anti-Semitic governments are conscious that their anti-Semitism creates internal problems for themselves.

The recent extension in Germany of the anti-Jewish regulations carries its own boomerang. One Jew out of five in Germany was already on relief before the new measures were taken, but there were still enough Jews in business life, possessed of a sufficient spirit of humanity toward their own race, to support an impressive charity.

But the new regulations will strangle the Jewish business community, cut off more Jews from the possibility of making a living and dry up the fount of German-Jewish charity. Moreover, the German annexation of Austria has augmented the number needing relief by hundreds of thousands.

A great number of people starving in the midst of any community is neither economically nor politically attractive. This must have been in the mind of General Goering when he declared that Vienna must be rid of its Jews by 1942!

It is a paradox that the world should give hospitality to people who were not only perfectly able to take care of themselves in their native land, but who would have sufficient money to establish themselves in other countries if their native lands would not sequester their savings—while on the other hand foreign citizens of the countries willing to extend hospitality to the refugees have their own funds blocked in these anti-Semitic countries too!

This is a paradox, and it is inconceivable! Since these anti-Semitic governments, theoretically at least, stand for the protection and recognition of private property, they must realize that only by some such cooperation as the one proposed can they hope to work out the problems they have themselves created.

And if, being asked to cooperate in a reasonable solution which overcomes the economic arguments they are accustomed to advance, and which does not raise, even, the political and ethical issues on which it will always be impossible for Fascism and democracy to agree—if, presented with such a possibility for cooperation, they refuse it—then, the world will have to draw, once and for all, the grimmest conclusion.

A CALL FOR LEADERSHIP

Obviously, this is not an ordinary business enterprise to be measured by daily experience and routine. Like all plans of great dimensions which involve the coordination of divergent elements, its success does not depend upon its commercial feasibility alone. It depends above all on the persons who are to carry it out. These persons must contribute confidence, energy, enthusiasm, endurance, and suavity in trying situations.

What Mr. Henry Morgenthau, Sr. said about the spirit in which he approached his task in Greece should be in the minds of all those who are concerned with the solution of the present refugee problem. He said:

"The dramatic element in large undertakings is the very first thing to be considered in the process of making them successful. Confidence and enthusiasm must be created at once. Imagination must be stirred. I had resolved to make every effort to have the Greeks and the rest of the world realize the magnitude and importance of this emergency, and the certainty and glory of mastering it."

No plan can be proposed that will do justice to the personal destiny of each and every refugee.

No plan can be proposed which will justify the forced migrations precipitated upon the world by the political policies of certain countries. No plan can be proposed that will not meet opposition in many quarters and from the most conflicting ideologies.

But whether any comprehensive plan will be proposed at all by any body of responsible people; whether any really grandiose attempt will be made to deal with this problem, depends in the final showdown, on whether there is a will anywhere in the world to deal with it.

The tragedy of the democracies is that their words are lofty, their gestures noble, but their deeds lag far behind. Of late years they have seemed paralyzed, and unable to mobilize the enormous resources which they still possess. They are in a mood of defeatism unjustified by the presence of insoluble economic problems. Our problem is to overcome our own weariness, and to fight our own callousness.

It is the firm belief of the author that the lot of the refugees can not only be ameliorated but that these victims of political and racial oppression can be made into assets for a score of countries.

It has happened before in history—very notably in our own history—for we have built a nation out of the thwarted dreams of Europe, and out of the will and necessity of economically frustrated peoples to find new homes and new existences, and the role of the political refugee in American history from William Penn to Carl Schurz—through all the great revolutionary epochs of Europe—has been an amazingly constructive one for us.

George Washington was only born in this country because his grandfather was a political refugee. William Penn fled to this country from the prisons of England, where his fight for freedom of conscience—the same fight that landed Otto Niemoeller in a Nazi concentration camp—kept him continually locked in various jails. Tom Paine may be called the original author of the Declaration of Independence, and he was twice a refugee in this country—once from the conservatism of England and once from the terror of the French Revolution. Woodrow Wilson's forebears were religious refugees from Ireland; the LaFollette family were Huguenot refugees; the Middle West was settled to its great advantage by many Forty-Eighters, and among those Forty-Eighters was the father of Justice Brandeis and the father of Adolph Ochs.

The political refugee brings to a new country a great psychological asset—gratitude for hospitality, and determination to survive.

Without a belief in the dignity of man, without

indignation against arbitrarily created human suffering and the will to overcome it, there is no democratic spirit.

With these ideas are integrated the fundamental concepts of our civilization. And so we are moved, not merely by pity for the exiles, but by the need to re-affirm our own beliefs, to take a stand for them, to re-capture the ground which our indifference has lost, lest all our precepts become hollow dogmas to which, at last, not even lip service will be given anywhere.

BIBLIOGRAPHY

League of Nations Documents

COMMITTEE ON INTERNATIONAL ASSISTANCE TO REFUGEES. *Report ... Submitted to the Council.* (C.2.M.2.1936.-XII.)
 Regulations concerning the juridical status of refugees, p. 15-18.

CONFÉRENCE INTERGOUVERNMENTALE POUR LE STATUT JURIDIQUE DES RÉFUGIÉS, GENEVA, 1928. ... *Documents Préparatoires et Procès Verbaux ... 28-30 Juin 1928. Arrangement et Accord du 30 Juin 1928.* (1930.XIII.1.) Text of the agreement, p. 191-195.

HOWLAND, CHARLES P. *Greek Refugee Settlement.* Geneva, League of Nations, 1926. (1926.II.32.)

INTERNATIONAL CONFERENCE FOR THE ADOPTION OF A CONVENTION CONCERNING THE STATUS OF REFUGEES COMING FROM GERMANY. *Final Act.* (C.75(a).M.30(a). 1938.XII.)

LEAGUE OF NATIONS. *Agreement with Regard to the Issue of Certificates of Identity to Russian Refugees. Signed at Geneva, July 5, 1922.* (Treaty Series, V. 13, p. 238-242.)

———. *Agreement Relating to the Issue of Identity Certificates to Russian and Armenian Refugees, Supplementing and Amending the Previous Arrangements Dated July 5, 1922, and May 31, 1924; Signed at Geneva, May 12, 1926.* (Treaty Series, V. 89, p. 48-52.)

LEAGUE OF NATIONS. *Letter of Resignation of James G. McDonald . . . Addressed to the Secretary-General . . . with an Annex Containing an Analysis of the Measures in Germany Against "Non-Aryan" and Their Effects in Creating Refugees.* (C.13.M.12.1936. XII and Annex.)

NANSEN, FRIDTJOF. *Russian Refugees; General Report on the Work Accomplished up to March 15, 1922.* (C.124.M.74.1922.)

————. *Report on the Work of the High Commission for Refugees . . .* (A.30.1923.XIII.i.e.IV.)

NANSEN INTERNATIONAL OFFICE FOR REFUGEES. *Report of the Governing Body.* Annual, 1932 to date.

Summarizes principal activities of the office from date of its establishment, April 1, 1931.

————. "Statutes." (In *Official Journal*, February, 1931, p. 308-311. [C.29.1931.XIII.])

Other Sources

BENTWICH, NORMAN. "The International Problem of Refugees." (In *Foreign Policy Reports*, February 12, 1936, p. 306-316.)

BOWMAN, ISAIAH, ED. *Limits of Land Settlement; A Report on Present-Day Possibilities.* New York, Council on Foreign Relations, 1937, 380 p. maps.

A report to the Tenth International Studies Conference, Paris, June 28–July 3, 1937, in which different regions suggested for settlement are discussed by Carl O. Sauer, Carl L. Alsberg, W. A. Mackintosh, Bruce Hopper, Owen Lattimore, Chen Han-seng, Karl J. Pelzer, Griffith Taylor, J. H. Wellington, and Isaiah Bowman.

HIGH COMMISSION FOR REFUGEES (JEWISH AND OTHER) COMING FROM GERMANY. *A Crisis in the University World*. London, Author, March 9, 1935.

———. *Report . . . of the Governing Body*. London, Author, 1934–1935.

Covers meetings May 2-4, November 1-2, 1934 and July 17, 1935.

HOWLAND, CHARLES P. "Greece and Her Refugees." (In *Foreign Affairs*, July, 1926, p. 613-623.)

MORGENTHAU, HENRY. *I Was Sent to Athens*. Garden City, Doubleday, 1929, 327 p.

NANSEN, FRIDTJOF. *Armenia and the Near East*. New York, Duffield, 1928, 324 p.

SIMPSON, SIR JOHN HOPE. "The League of Nations and Refugees." (In *Fortnightly*, February, 1938, p. 225-230.)

WALDECK, COUNTESS. "The Great New Migration." (In *Foreign Affairs*, April, 1937, p. 537-546.)